HOW TO THINK LIKE A Billionaire

HOW TO THINK LIKE A Billionaire

PRADEEP THAKUR

Published by
PRABHAT PAPERBACKS
An imprint of Prabhat Prakashan Pvt. Ltd.
4/19 Asaf Ali Road,
New Delhi-110002 (INDIA)
e-mail: prabhatbooks@gmail.com

ISBN 978-93-5521-130-9
HOW TO THINK LIKE A BILLIONAIRE
by Pradeep Thakur

Edition
First, 2022

Price
₹ 250 (Rupees Two Hundred Fifty Only)

Printed at
Sanjay Printers, Sahibabad

Dedicated with love to my wife KIRAN, who was always supportive during my course of full-time writing, and my forever encouraging sons—PRABHAKAR, PUSHKAR, and BHASKAR

Author's Note

Have you ever thought—Yes, I can become an affluent person! Perhaps you had. This is the first and most important condition to be a rich person. If you only think without reasoning and tell your mind, "Yes, I can be rich," it won't have any positive effect. Until this notion is understood, one can not become rich, as this is the beginning of the journey that will change one's entire life for the better.

There are more pessimistic than optimistic elements in our education system, society, and intellect. The Indian system is not the only one restricted to this thought, as this truth trapped the entire world. Our socio-economic structure is built in such a manner that it forces a substantial section of society to become pessimists.

This is not true at all. If the idea of "a group of the prosperous elite" exits, it is because of the mindlessness of a few people who have accepted their poverty without any reason and this is why they don't even try to become a part of this group. The fact is there is no such elite group. Only a few of the rich are born wealthy. Most of them have made themselves rich. If you ask any rich and successful person that how 'did they become rich' there answer will be the same; they started trusting themselves that they will become successful and famous one day. This book presents the opportunity to know about many such people.

In general, people who aren't rich tend to believe they cant become rich; it's a game of luck that only a few can succeed at. Whenever you discuss the idea of becoming rich with your close ones, what answer do you get? Wasn't it like 'stop daydreaming' and 'be realistic'! I am not saying anything surprising, nor am I unraveling any secret. This is a universal psychological fact. Most people think the same way and that this is how it is meant to be.

However, it is not true at all. A group of prosperous elites exists due to the mindlessness of a few people who accept their poverty and give up on trying to join this group. The fact is there is no such elite group. Only a few rich are born wealthy, and most of them have made themselves rich. If you ask any wealthy and successful person how 'did they become rich?' their answer will be the same; "They believed in themselves to create a successful life." This book will allow you to know more about such successful ad wealthy people.

First, you should accept you have not thought about this topic sincerely and then ask yourself, 'Can I will be rich? This is indeed a complex thought process; therefore, don't be reluctant or hasty to go to the roots of your thoughts. Keep yourself calm and look into ideas from an entirely circumstantial perspective. Circumstantial perspective is the mentality when we look at things unbiased, like a deponent. This is a condition where you look at an event without participating. Once you start doing this, the obstacles on your road to success that you had raised yourself will become clear. You might also feel that you had never thought about this very seriously. Otherwise, you would have started your journey a long time ago. Anyway, if this journey is meant to begin now, so be it. Better late than never.

I am sure this book will be inspirational to all its readers on their road to success and wealth.

Contents

1

WHERE TO START THE JOURNEY OF PROSPERITY

"The journey of a thousand miles starts with one small step."

—Lao Tzu

"The way to start is to stop talking and start doing."

Walt Disney

Co-founder of Walt Disney

Renowned American cartoonist

Do you want to be rich? Obviously, the answer will be 'yes'; otherwise, why would you be excited to read this book? But the biggest hurdle to achieving this dream is your mental conditioning. After all, who does not want to be rich! But your journey will not start merely by thinking. The obvious question in everybody's mind is: "From where do I start?" Before this, you must answer, "What is your definition of rich?" Do you think that being rich means raising your income? Most of the people consider this as a definition of being rich. Very few aim to become millionaires and billionaires. Now, it is evident that your mind must be thinking about the point of start.

Yes, I can become rich!

This statement seems intriguing at; first happens to everybody. But ask your mind patiently, Can I become rich? Don't be hasty in decision-making because this is the first and most important condition of the process. The answer to this question will change your life forever. It won't serve the purpose if you can convince yourself that you can be rich without appropriate thinking. This is the starting point of your journey.

Why am I stressing on this point? The reason is a bit complicated as well as psychological. As I mentioned before, the structures of socio-economic development of the entire world are such that it forces a majority of the population to pessimism. Yes, our condition forces us into this negative mindset that it's not in my control to become rich. What answer did you get whenever you tried to share the idea of becoming rich with your close ones? Wasn't it something like being realistic? And this answer is not new; we all got this from our friends and family. It is a universal psychological fact. This is the perception of most people, which they also consider practical. But this is not true at all. We all can become affluent and successful; we just have to change our mindset. Five out of hundreds are born with a silver spoon; the rest of the wealthy and successful people achieve their dream with a positive and strong mindset.

Here you will understand why I told you to think calmly and patiently. Let me warn you again not to take this matter casually, however it will look casual at first. Simple, Let me ask you one question, "Do you want to be rich?" to answer this question on a serious note, you will go through a complicated thought process. Don't panic; keep yourself composed and examine your thoughts with a circumstantial perspective. If you are wondering what is the circumstantial condition? The circumstantial situation is the mental state where you look at things like a witness without being a part of the event.

Once you start doing that, you will be more and more apparent of the obstacle put in by yourself in your path. You might also feel that you might not have raised any barriers for yourself; you are in denial. And If it is not valid, your journey would have started a long time ago.

It would be best to convince yourself that you could be rich and that this journey is not as difficult as it seemed. It would be best to tell yourself that the possibility is not as far-fetched as it looks. As you had not looked into things from a precise point of view, things were blurry. Now you are ready to look into your reality without any biases, and I hope things are getting a lot clearer. As days pass naturally, you will be able to see new opportunities, which are shadowed by your negative presumptions (things such as I cannot be rich, and fortune only favors a few).

It's true! Since your subconscious was pessimistic for so long, you could not identify the opportunities. When these negative presumptions and biases have disappeared from your eyes and mind, you will witness all your deeds and distinguish between right and wrong

In the third chapter, we shall discuss the art of self-suggestion, which will help you understand and develop your capacity for inner understanding or understanding of your sixth sense. Out of all the natural beings, only humans have this sixth sense apart from the five senses– ear (listening), eyes (vision), skin (touch), nose (smell), and tongue (taste), and this sense gives the financial perspective to become rich. This sixth sense is the secret of all the millionaires to achieve great success. Yes, nature has blessed this sixth sense to you too, but you have not yet recognized it.

Success is not challenging as accepting defeat

For most people, failure has become a way of life. Its psychological effect is so powerful that it becomes a habit and challenging to get rid of. This inferiority complex creeps in individuals because of their social conditioning, which does not allow them to expect great things from life. In the journey to becoming rich, one should accept that success is more challenging to achieve than failure short; it is just a different kind of mental programming. Without which, we cannot read the signal of our subconscious mind.

Isn't it possible that failures are only an of different complicated situations? Think for a moment, "Why? Every time you try hard and still miss your target. You throw away golden opportunities; you miss opportunities to meet people who could help you climb the ladder of success. You discard every idea that might have yielded positive results. You do the same thing repeatedly, which takes you closer to failure.

Will I say failure is an achievement? Otherwise, why would you readily accept defeat again and again? Your subconscious considers failure something natural and gives you the strength to endure repeated failures, and you keep trying to become successful. So, Isn't failure an achievement?

We shall discuss the role of subconsciousness in detail in the next chapter. We shall focus on an in-depth analysis of those reasons (which are mere excuses) that prevent people from believing that they can be rich and will help you understand the abstract of our discussion.

Were the days good?

You must have come across this statement a million times, and it was easy to be successful in the past. Those were the good old days. While the reality is just the opposite, becoming successful is getting easier every day, and it will continue to be like this. And many use this phrase as an instrument to validate our mental inertness and unknowingly keep encouraging acceptance of our failure. Now, the rich people are not only confined to America, Europe, or any other western country; many billionaires are continuously rising from Asian countries. And the noticeable thing is that most of them are from the young generation and achieved their success on their own.

According to the latest market research report of New World Wealth, India has 14,800 multi-millionaires, which places it at the eighth position in the world, with Mumbai ranking first with 2700 multi-millionaires.

According to this survey, the total number of multi-millionaires globally was 495000 until June 2014. America (183500) is at the top of the list. Don't; be surprised when you see China (26600)in the second position. Germany (25400) is in the third, once a ruler of the world, the United Kingdom (21700) was in the fourth spot; followed by Japan (21000), Switzerland (18300), Hong Kong (15400), Russia (11700) and Brazil (10300) at the fifth, sixth, seventh, ninth and tenth spot. But only 0.68 percent of the total population of the 7.29 billion globally are multi-millionaire.

This is why it seems like a group of the prosperous elite. But the truth is that hundreds of new people are joining this club every day. According to the above survey, from 2007 to 2013, the annual growth rate of the new multi-millionaires was only 8% because of the global recession. However, over the next ten years(2013–2023), the growth rate is expected to be 28 percent, meaning there will be 1,38,600 new members per year or 379 per day who will join this elite club.

Now it is easier to become rich

The above survey clearly shows that getting rich is becoming easier every day; however, many people believe that it was more accessible in the past. To justify their inaction and failure, these people cite that competition is rising, making business difficult.

Despite the recession, the number of billionaires has more than doubled to 1646 in the last five years (2009:2014).

Refer Table

Year	No. of Billionaires	The Net Worth of the Group (in Billion)
2000	470	898
2001	538	18
2002	497	15
2003	476	14
2004	587	19
2005	691	22
2006	793	26
2007	946	35
2008	1,125	44
2009	793	24
2010	1,011	36
2011	1210	45
2012	1,226	46
2013	1426	54
2014	1,645	64

In 2014, economic disparity reached its worst level since 1820, which concerns organizations like Organization for Economic Co-Operation and Development. The American capitalistic policies are the reason for this gap, and economists all over the globe are striving to bridge the gap. This is the biggest challenge of the 21st century, and we should take every measure possible to meet it. The next chapter will reveal the touching stories of business leaders who overcame all obstacles to succeed.

Excuses for not becoming rich

How are you feeling now? Now, do you believe that if the person born in adversity can be rich, so can you? Do their stories inspire you? If yes, let's begin with knowing some obstacles that stop you from achieving it.

I am too young: if you are young, you will generally think that this is the age to enjoy not to worry about money, as you are too young to think about it.

Then why are you holding this book? Because this book will help you spend your days reading some exciting stories and novels.

As Swami Vivekananda said, 'wake up and start doing and don't stop till your goal is achieved.' It is possible that you must have read or heard it somewhere. I am listing some young billionaires that live by Swami Vivekanand's quote,

The co-founder of Apple, Steve Jobs, became a millionaire at 23. The director of movies like 'Jurassic Park' and 'Indiana Jones became a billionaire when he was 35 years old. Forbes reported in March 2015that, out of 1645 billionaires, 31 were under 40 years old.

Name	Company	Age	Net Worth
Perenna Kei	LoganProperty Holding	24 years	1.3 billion USD
Dustin Moskowitch	Facebook employee	29 years	6.8 billion USD
Mark Zuckerberg	Founder Facebook	29 years	28.5 billion USD
Anton Kathrein Jr.	Kathrein Verke AG	29 years	1.35 billion USD
Drew Houston	Dropbox	30 years	1.3 billion USD
Scott Duncan	Enterprise product partner	31 years	6.3 billion USD
Eduardo Saverin	Co-founder facebook	31 years	4.21 billion USD
Yang Hui Yan	Country garden	32 years	6.9 billion USD
Marie Besnier Beauvalot	Lactalis	33 years	2.7 billion USD
Sean Parker	Napster founder	34 years	2.4 billion USD
Julia Oetker	Dr. Augusta Oetkar KG	35 years	1.65 billion USD
Robert Pera	Ubiquity network	35 years	2.7 billion USD

Ayaman Hariri	Director of Southie Ogor	35 years	12.2 billion USD
Naruatsu Baba	Colopal Smartphone	36 years	2.2 billion USD
Von Bauer	Baeur media group	36 years	3 billion USD
Lawerence Ho	Melco Crown Entertainment	36 years	3 billion USD
Yoshikazu Tanaka	Grid social networking games	37 years	1.3 billion USD
Jack Dorse	Twitter	37 years	2.2 billion USD
Alessandro Santo Domingo Davila	Quadrant capital advertisers	37 years	11.1 billion USD
Jan Koum	WhatsApp	38 Years	6.8 billion USD
Nicholas Woodman	Go Pro	38 Years	1.3 billion USD
Chase Coleman-III	Tiger Global Management	38 Years	1.6 billion USD
Yasaku Maezawa	Jojotown	38 Years	1.25 billion USD
Rahel Blocher	Ems-Chemie	38 Years	1.25 billion USD
John Oringer	Shutter stock	39 Years	1.35 billion USD

Liu Kiangdong	JD.com	39 Years	2.7 billion USD
Ryan Kawanog	Relativity media	39 years	1 billion USD

I am too old: If you have crossed fifty and feel like you are too old to try, you need to rethink. The founder brothers of multinational food chain McDonald's were also trapped in the old mentality. They became the richest in San Bernardino (California) with a hard struggle, but unexpected success made them complacent. Most people mistake comfort as the ultimate goal and give up their mantra of hard work as the key to his success. Since the McDonald brothers had no heir, they began to think, 'who should we earn for now.' Why should we work only to pay taxes to the government? What was the result of this?

Ray Kroc, a 52-year-old man with diabetes and arthritis, snatched the crown away from the McDonald brothers. Despite having his gall bladder removed, he kept himself busy until he died in his eighties and set up McDonald's as a massive chain with 7,778 outlets across the globe to 31st March 1984 with 2.20 billion USD revenue.

In 2013, the McDonald Corporation was enjoying a profit of 5.58 billion dollars over the 28.11 billion dollar business with more than 35000 outlets spread across the globe and an average of 680 million customers served daily.

Kroc used to say, 'When you are green, you are growing; when you ripe, you rot.' He adhered to this philosophy till his last breath. This is an inspiration for many grown men.

Napoleon Hill, a renowned self-help author, noted that most people commence their journey to riches after 40. He gathered this information by surveying thousands of wealthy individuals. If you haven't yet been lucky, you shouldn't be depressed. Hopefully, now you will have the opportunity to reap the rewards of your efforts. Ray Kroc gives inspiration even to the physically weak and afflicted with diseases.

I don't have capital: You must have heard people say they don't have enough money. Lack of capital seems the biggest hurdle to most people. But the most affluent person has not a single penny when they begin their successful journey with two essential elements; a positive mentality and a good business idea.

You must have seen lots of businesses shut down every day. When you look deep, you will find that they lacked in two things : business strategy and the unwillingness to learn from their errors despite having the capital. Such people are engulfed in self-admiration and cannot see their own mistakes. If anyone points out their mistakes, they don't take it in the right spirit.

I am not educated: Thomas Edison quit his school before he turned 16. Bill Gates (Microsoft), Steve Jobs (Apple), Larry Ellison (Oracle), Mark Zuckerberg (Facebook), and many other greats quit their studies midway. Still, they became technical and business tycoons in their respective fields. This proves that a college degree does not guarantee success.

I don't have any exceptional talent: Most successful people cannot identify their exceptional talent at the beginning of their careers. In retrospect, it's hard to imagine they would become so rich and famous.

In 1966 Guinness's book of world records announced Jean Paul Getty, the founder of Getty Oil Company, was the wealthiest private citizen with 1.2 billion dollars (equivalent to 8.7 billion dollars in 2014). At the time of his death in 1972, Getty's net worth was 2 billion dollars (equivalent to 8.30 billion dollars in 2014). Getty often used to say I was not born a businessperson for sure. But many people blame the lack of talents for their failure. The exciting part is that they accredit the success of others to good fortune. 'I had also labored hard, but he was fortunate since he was born with exceptional talent. Instead of realizing their own mistake, acknowledging and praising the hard work and dedication, and learning the art to be successful, we blame our luck for our failures and keep crying that God did not make us talented enough.

But the truth is that nature has given unique talents to every living being. Man is the most developed of all the living beings, he is born with more qualifications, and everybody has some exceptional talent. It is just that successful people cane embracealise that talent, nourish them, and keep climbing the ladder of success. Look around yourself, and you will find that every successful person has talent, and when you go into the depth, you will know that they continuously polish their talent.

Read this quote by Steve Jobs, and try to understand the gist:

"For the past 33 years, every morning I look at myself and ask: would I be doing what I will do today if I knew today was my last day? ... And if the answer is a no for many days, I feel something has to be changed."

You will spend a large part of your life at work. In other words, if you want to feel satisfied, you should do what you think is great; doing something you love is the only way to do it well. Be persistent in your search for it, don't compromise. Once you feel it, you'll find it.

I don't have enough energy in me: The person who keeps praying for success comes across a successful person closely and sees that they have the power to work. Is this the kind of energy needed to be successful? It is the difference between those who are successful and those who are unsuccessful. We need a certain amount of mental and physical energy to accomplish any task. When neither is present, depression occurs.

Is the energy level different for each individual? ? Is this some vicious circle that can't be broken? Most people look at it because they can't experience their life force. Unless you light the fire within you, how will you fan it? Humans are a powerhouse of infinite life force. Every day we see people do wonders. The computer works like a human brain; however, the computer's analyzing and processing power is limited to a hard disk, but the human brain has no limitation.

Let us compare a scholar with a scholar? One has physical strength while the other has mental strength. Why is a scholar physically not strong as a wrestler, or why is a wrestler mentally not as strong as a wrestler? Human being has mental as well as physical capacities. The part you work on will emerge more powerful. Hence, it is evident that we can enhance our strengths with a good workout.

There is one more force, the inner power of your soul; we can also call it the life force. We must understand that our likings are different from others. Everybody does not like everything. So whatever excites you depends on your nature, which is your life force. Try to test it very calmly and keep nourishing slowly. You will find the strength you were looking for, and once you've seen it, don't let it vanish; your road to success will get more precise with every passing day. In simple terms, we call it 'The Awakening.'

Behind every success story, there is Awakening. It makes your mind and body move after your soul. This will combine the three forces, and whatever you do will be a success. The above Steve Jobs quote is all about that. Now you need to ask yourself – do you love what you do? If yes, success is not far from you, and if not, you must look for something you love to do. The later you find it, the farther success goes from you.

Afraid of failures: We human beings are not even scared of facing the hardest natural calamities due to the scientific strength of our brains. However, we fear failure. Fear is so overwhelming that, as humankind progresses, many people are getting engulfed in it. What's the reason? Why is a large section of society being entrapped in it?

When we dig deep, we find unsuccessful perspective is transferred from one generation to another, just like hereditary and genetic traits. In the name of imparting practical knowledge, society and family fill the tender minds of a younger age with the horrors of failure. As a result, when we try to climb the ropes of success, this fear pulls us back to the back of our minds. This fear of failure is at the foundation of our thought process. Since you can't repair the faulty foundation without destroying it, getting rid of this fear at the roots of your thought is very tough, demolishing the lifestyle. This fear prevents the natural mental growth of our mind like a virus stops the working system of the entire computer.

So, what should we do? Is it possible to change a human mind like a computer's software? Well. It is possible but not as easy as changing a computer's software. It is so because of no manual guides for the mental process of a human being. The human body is not a non-living being like the hardware of a computer where you can install a new version without the machine knowing about it. Of course, the human brain and computer software function in a very similar manner. Computers also work on reasoning, and hence the preparation of new software for it is a complicated process like feeding new recreating the reason or else software of a human brain. We shall do a detailed discussion about this later, but for now, it is essential to understand that the brain's software was corrupted, and we need to debug it. It is up to you if you want to do it yourself or with the help of this book.

Other Excuses: The road to success is not as hard as our presumptions and biases. For example: whatever I did, I failed. Here the question that arises is, did you ever try to contemplate? Why did your trials fail? Most people are unable to answer correctly. Why? Because they cannot identify their specialty and keep doing things that are not by their nature. Have you ever wondered that you never fail when you do something through your heart or soul? Then look at your mistakes in a new light and walk only on that path your heart accepts naturally. Do you know that the fraud committed by honest people is caught in the first instance itself, while it is tough to see a dishonest man?

Life is a mirror of beliefs

To improve your financial conditions, search for an appropriate job, get a salary hike, increase your income manifolds, and keep yourself healthy and fit, you need to change your life with immense passion. You need to treat yourself harshly, embrace the right attitude and change the basics of your ideology. You should make these habits a goal in your life. If you want to be rich, you will have to put this determination and passion at the top of your life.

This is because our life mirrors our faith, point of view, and beliefs. We need to change our lives to the ones we dream about. Otherwise, nothing will change. Then it's all talks and nothing else. Once you have decided to change your life, there is no need to look back. You will have to live every moment with your ambition, and once you start doing that, all your shortcomings will vanish. All the needful improvements will come naturally and ultimately will become your nature. Then you do not feel like someone trying to be rich; instead, you will start living in its spirit.

To accomplish any task, you will have to develop your laborious side strategically. It is not easy, and at the same time, it is not complex as well. Labor means to try, and one who tries is called laborious. Whatever your trade might be, you must have a clear vision of what you want to achieve? And only dreaming about it will give you nothing. As mentioned above, your determination should be so strong, and your vision should be so clear that it becomes a part of nature, and then when you do something naturally, you will not have to put extra effort to do it. Eventually, it will be done, and you will not even notice it.

When this happens, you can say that you are becoming a natural hard worker, and as you keep on polishing it, your aim will become more evident to you. Step by step, your goal will come nearer to you, and gradually you will realize this journey itself is your goal. Although this will look casual to you at that time for the entire idle world, you will become extraordinary. And it is called the journey of success. Only those courageous enough to leap of faith and start walking can become successful. Those who choose to sit keep on sitting.

There is a Sanskrit shloka:

उद्यमेन हि सिध्यन्ति कार्याणि न मनोरथैः ।
न हि सुप्तस्य सिंहस्य प्रविशन्ति मुखे मृगाः

Work gets accomplished by effort, industry, not merely by wishing. The animals don't enter a sleeping lion's mouth.

Completing the job that is the accomplishment of goals can be done only by working; even a lion has to hunt a deer for food. Oh yes! There is one famous quote: "You can't go to heaven unless you die" in other words, you can't feel the joys of heaven unless you try till near death. Only your determination and passion can drive you to work efficiently to achieve your goal.

Let me tell you a story. Once a pupil said to his teacher, "Sir, please tell me a way to enlightenment. I have been waiting for a long time for this." The teacher felt his student is very eager to attain enlightenment. He took the pupil to a river and submerged his head in the water. The student started shaking in moments, shook his teacher's hands, and took out his head with one blow. His face had gone red due to a shortage of breath. He kept looking at his teacher in surprise. "How are you feeling?" The teacher asked, "What was it that you wanted when your head was underwater?" "Breath," the pupil answered, taking deep breaths. The teacher said, "Absolutely, for now, breathe." The pupil looked at the teacher, surprised, and asked, "But I was asking for the way to enlightenment." The teacher replied, "Unless you are dying, you don't know the value of breath, and till you take your head out of the water with all power, you can't breathe. Similarly, when you yearn for the knowledge, you will get it."

Now you also make a decision. Recite this poem again and again as it will help you grow your determination:

लहरों से डरकर नौका पार नहीं होती
कोशिश करने वालों की हार नहीं होती।

नन्ही चींटी जब दाना लेकर चलती है
चढ़ती दीवारों पर, सौ बार फिसलती है।
मन का विश्वाश रगों में साहस भरता है
चढ़कर गिरना, गिरकर चढ़ना न अखरता है।
आखिर उसकी मेहनत बेकार नहीं होती,
कोशिश करने वालों की हार नहीं होती।

डुबकियां सिन्धु में गोताखोर लगाता है,
जा जाकर खाली हाथ लौटकर आता है।
मिलते नहीं सहज ही मोती गहरे पानी में,
बढ़ता दुगना उत्साह इसी हैरानी में।
मुट्ठी उसकी खाली हर बार नहीं होती,
कोशिश करने वालों की हार नहीं होती।

असफलता एक चुनौती है , इसे स्वीकार करो,
क्या कमी रह गई, देखो और सुधार करो।

जब तक न सफल हो , नींद चैन को त्यागो तुम,
संघर्ष का मैदान छोड़कर मत भागो तुम।
कुछ किए बिना ही जय-जयकार नहीं होती,
कोशिश करने वालों की हार नहीं होती।

Summary

Believe that you can be successful: Have faith in yourself. It is possible when you get rid of baseless thoughts and drive in a positive attitude. Hurdles are bound to come, but you have to stay put in your job with all sincerity– not for once or multiple times; you have to be continuous in your efforts, and for that, you must fall in love with your job (goal), only then will you be able to convince others to lend a helping hand to you.

Things will not change by themselves: Success does not come packaged in a golden box. One has to work hard to achieve his targets. You must step out like a lion in a jungle, and you need to chase your target. Therefore you must build the courage to challenge your conditions and keep moving towards your goal without caring for difficulties. You must remember that every step further you take shortens the distance between you and success. Never make the mistake of jumping too high. Put your efforts further with complete confidence and caution. Each step will show you the path ahead.

The only strong determination can change your life: Always keep fanning the fire of perseverance and passion for achieving your goals. The higher this fire rises, the sooner you burn your inner inhibitions. Make a list of all the baseless assumptions that create a hurdle in your way. Look at them closely. You can't defeat this enemy unless you keep a close watch on them. Identifying these shortcomings will also help you identify your strengths and then be able to overcome all the obstacles. Every successful man tries to get rid of their inhibitions in their way. This is why they have complete faith in themselves and their strategies. This is why they don't deviate from their path despite all the obstructions. With strong determination, they keep riding the victory vehicle.

Empower yourself to chase your dreams: you can be successful only when you have a plan. If you don't dare to take the necessary steps to achieve your dreams, it is not your dream. Your natural dream will make you chase it with all your passion, and you will smell the scent of success nearer with every step. Therefore develop the art to listen and respond to the calls of your subconscious. Bring your thoughts into your life and keep moving further. You will feel success walking behind you.

❑

2

HOW DID THE BILLIONAIRES OVERCOME THE OBSTACLES

"Your present circumstances don't determine where you can go; they merely determine where you start."

—Nido Qubein

Businessperson, motivational speaker,

And president of High Point University

"You must take personal responsibility. You cannot change the circumstances, the seasons, or the wind, but you can change yourself. That is something you have charge of."

—Emanuel James "Jim" Rohn

American entrepreneur, author and motivational speaker

Can financial disparity or other socio-geographical conditions stop somebody from becoming rich? The people who will say yes could be huge in number because this thought has dug its deep root almost all over the world, but the rising number of billionaires is enough to demolish this idea. The main point is : why do only a few become rich while most of us fail? Adverse conditions or lack of opportunities might create hurdles, but they can never stop somebody forever from becoming successful.

Many have not only challenged this notion but also proved it wrong. It isn't easy to narrow down the list, but let us look at fifteen business people who were once like us and did not give in to the views of society and family. Instead, they challenged their circumstances. They did not wait to get lucky but made their luck with hard work and determination; they did not get euphoric by initial success but continuously kept raising the bar for themselves till they became a world standard. They not only became billionaires but an inspiration to many of us. So, here are the short stories of those legends!

The son of a bartender Kenny Trout (1.5 Billion Dollars)

Kenny Trout was born in 1948 to a very modest family in Mount Vernon, Illinois. His father was a bartender. He sold life insurance to complete his studies at Southern Illinois University. In 1988, he founded a telecommunication company named Excel Communications that used multi-level marketing for long-distance phone calls.

A couple of years after the company went public, Trout merged it with Teleglobal (Canada) for 3.5 billion dollars. Later, in 2005 it was taken over by B.S.N.L International (a subsidiary company of Tata Group's Tata communications). Trout is currently enjoying his retirement and is founder-director at Winstar Farm, a Thoroughbred 'horse farm in Versailles, Kentucky. As calculated by Forbes, his net worth was 1.5 billion dollars on 26th October 2014.

Howard Schultz, the son of a truck driver (2.2 Billion Dollars)

Schultz was born in a Jewish family in Brooklyn, New York, on 19th July 1953. His father was an Ex-United states army trooper and truck driver and lived with his family in a multi-story residential society made for the poor's. After various struggles, he got a football scholarship and managed to pay for his education at the North Michigan University. He was the first member of his family to go to college. After completing his graduation (commerce) in 1971, he started his professional career as a trainee sales clerk at Xerox Corporation. In 1979, he became a general manager for a Swedish drip coffee maker manufacturer. In 1981 during a customer survey, he got so impressed by the business structure and future possibilities of a customer, Starbucks Coffee, that he got after the partners to join it. Then he left his well-established job and started working as an employee for a meager salary and took the risk of becoming an executive partner. He became the CEO in 1987, and five years later, in 1997, Schultz made the company public the total number of coffee stores was 140 (total revenue of 73.5 million dollars. Before anyone could realize it, Starbucks became the largest coffee house chain globally, with 21,600 branches across 63 countries till November 2014. The total revenue in the financial year 2013 was 14.89 billion dollars. In March 2013, Forbes calculated Schultz's net worth of 2.2 billion dollars.

Son of a plumber, Kenneth Langone (2.5 Billion Dollars)

Langone's father was a plumber, and his mother used to work in a cafeteria in the Roselyn Heights, Nassau County, in rural New York. He was born on 16th September 1935. Not only did his parents mortgage their home, but Langone himself had to work as a butcher's assistant, caddie, and do manual labor to pay for his education at Bucknell University (Lewisburg, Pennsylvania). Then he attended New York University Stern School of Business the night while he worked full time during the day.

He started his professional career in R.W Pressprich, a financial services company. In 1968 he convinced the tycoon Ross Parrot to make Electronics Data System public, and with this enormous success, he became the head of Pressprich in 1969. He made a huge financial success by establishing a venture capital firm, Invented associates. But Langone is widely known for his home-based product and services firm Home Depot. His net worth in September 2014 was 2.5 billion dollars.

Oprah Winfrey, the single mother (2.9 Billion Dollars)

Oprah Winfrey (29 January 1954) was born to a teenage mother who worked as a housemaid. In a pig barn, she spent six years with her grandmother in Kosciusko in Mississippi, America, and had to go through terrible times. Later, when she lived with her mother in Milwaukie, she was molested by her cousins and family friend at nine. She tried to revolt and fled many times but ultimately became an unmarried mother at fourteen. The premature baby died in infancy.

When she was about to be sent to a rehabilitation center for lewd behavior, her father came forward to rescue her and support her. Oprah also reshaped herself and started her education at Nashville High School (Nashville, Tennessee). She became the most popular girl in her school and became part of the school's speech team, and stood second in the country in dramatic descriptions. Then she won the Speech competition and got into Tennessee State University with a full scholarship.

At the age of 17, she won the Miss Black Tennessee Beauty Pageant and accepted a temporary job proposal at the local black radio station W.V.C.O.L. After completing her studies; she became the youngest news anchor of W.L.L.C TV. She began presenting the news bulletin at 6 in the evening on W.J.Z TV in 1976 in Baltimore. Then in 1983, she started presenting the least popular tv show, A.M Chicago, and it became the most popular tv show overrunning all local programs. From 8th September 1986 (till 2011), this became the historic national one-hour program, 'The Oprah Winfrey Show,' and Oprah became the 'queen of media, the wealthiest Black American, and the most outstanding philanthropist in the history of America. On 2nd February 2015, Forbes estimated her net worth to be 3 billion dollars.

Shahid Khan, the dishwasher (4.6 Billion Dollars)

When 16-year-old Shahid Khan, who was born in a middle-class family in Lahore on 18th July 1950, arrived at Illinois University: Urbana Champaign to pursue graduation in Electrical engineering, he had to spend his first night in a small 2-dollar room in Y.M.C. He started working as a dishwasher at 1.2 dollars an hour. After completing his studies, he soon began to work in Flex N Gate, a motor part production company, where he became the Director. In 1978, he raised a bank loan of 50000 dollars to form a car bumpers manufacturing unit called Bumper Works. In 1980 he was able to buy his employer Flex N Gate and started supplying bumpers to the three largest car manufacturers (the big three): Ford, General Motors, and Chrysler.

In 1984, he began supplying a small number of bumpers for Toyota pickups and became the sole supplier for pickup in 1987 and 1989 for Toyota America. In 2012, Khan was operating 48 production units in America and other countries, and the annual revenue generation was 3 billion dollars. In January 2012, Khan purchased a National Football League team, Jacksonville Jaguars, for 76 million dollars. In July 2013, he bought the English Football League Championship Team, Fulham F.C, for 15:20 Million Pounds.

In September 2014, Forbes asserted his net worth of 4.6 billion dollars, and Shahid Khan became the wealthiest Pakistani.

The son of poor immigrants, Kirk Kerkorian (3.9 Billion Dollars)

Kirk was born on 6th June 1917 in an extremely poor Armenian immigrant family in Fresno, California, and Kirk had to quit his education in eighth grade to support his parents financially. Under the tutelage of his elder brother, he became a skilled boxer and won the Pacific amateur welterweight championship. During the Second World War, he was compelled to join the army and train as an aircraft pilot, and he got his commercial license within six months and joined the British Royal Air Force.

When the war was over, Kirk put in all his savings (5000 dollars) to buy a Cesena (four-seater) aircraft and started working as a general pilot. He got addicted to gambling during his trips to Las Vegas and started a chartered flight service for the gamblers and started operating between Las Vegas and Los Angeles. He paid Trans international airlines 60000 dollars for this.

Going through all the ups and downs in his business, in 1962, he bought 80 Acre land on the Las Vegas strip for 960 thousand dollars, where he built the Luxury hotel and casino, Caesar's Palace. In 1967 he bought 80-acre land for 5 million dollars in paradise road (Las Vegas) and made it the most significant international hotel. In 1968, he sold Caesar's Palace for 9 million dollars. In 1969, he bought the metro Goldwin Mayor (MGM) studios, where he built the M.G.M Grand hotel and casino. The troubles did not stop ever despite his progress. On 21st November 1980, the original M.G.M studio caught fire and turned into ashes. Eighty-seven people lost their lives in that event. But this could not dishearten Kerkorian. Within eight months, he rebuilt a brand new M.G. M

Studios and sold it in 1986 for 594 million dollars and was renamed Bally's Las Vegas.

Then Kerkorian created a storm in the automobile industry through his strategic investment and shareholding. Be it Chryslers or for motors or General motors, Kerkorian intimidated everybody. In September 2007, his net worth was 16 billion dollars, which came down to 3.9 billion dollars in September 2013 due to the recession.

The street boy, John Paul Dejoria (4 Billion Dollars)

In the Echo Park neighborhood of Los Angeles, California, John Paul Jones Dejoria was born as the second son of an Italian immigrant father and a Greek immigrant mother on April 13, 1944. His parents divorced by the time he was two years old, and at nine, he began selling Christmas cards and newspapers with his older brother to support his family. He had just reached High School when his single mother could not support him, and he and his brother were sent to an East Los Angeles foster home. He joined a group of vagabonds but decided to change his life when his maths teacher's words 'he can never achieve anything' motivated him.

Dejoria spent two years in the Navy after completing high school in 1967. After that, he worked in various jobs, from nightguard to an insurance agent, to entering the world of hair care in Redken Laboratories, which is now a well-established brand in the L'Oreal group.

He founded John Paul Mitchell System (Hawaii) in 1980 with his friend Paul Mitchell and a loan of 700 dollars. He roamed in his car and sold shampoo door to door. He co-founded Patron Spirits (Mexico) in 1989 and started tequila of sale; in 1992, he co-founded 'House of Blues", a chain of live music concert halls and restaurants, and bought shares in Madagascar Oil (South Africa).

Forbes had calculated Dojeria's net worth to be 4 billion dollars in September 2013.

Do Won Chang (4 Billion Dollars)

Do Won Chong, born in a modest family (20th March 1941) in South Korea, worked hard in a coffee shop. He saved some money from his job and arrived in Los Angeles (Southern California) in 1981 when he was 18 years old. He worked three jobs simultaneously for his livelihood. He noticed that garment merchants travel in extensive and costly cars. Hence in 1984, he opened 'Fashion 21,' a 900 sq feet ready made garment shop in Highland Park (Los Angeles) with his wife, Jin Souk.

He targeted the South Korean community, and in the first year itself, the revenue generation was

700 thousand dollars. He opened a new store every six months, and the chain was renamed 'Forever 21'. By 2013, it has spread to 480 places worldwide, and the annual revenue generation has risen to 3.7 billion dollars. Forbes had calculated the net worth of Chang and Souk together to be 5.4 billion dollars.

The old rags tie tailor–Ralph Lauren

Ralph Lauren was born in The Bronx (14th October 1939), New York City, to house painters Jewish immigrants from Pinsk, Belarus. Lauren quit his graduation to serve in the army, and later, he left the military to join Brooks Brothers, the oldest men's garment chain, as a sales clerk. Later he became a salesman in a tie company. He developed a liking for European ties in 1966 when he was 26 years old. When the company rejected his designs, he started tailoring ties from old rags in a drawer in the Empire state building. When sales improved, he took a loan from a garment manufacturer to start his tie store under the brand 'Polo.' He started his polo boutique in radio drives, Beverly Hills. After winning the Coty award, he brought in the small sleeve Polo Shirts and women's fashion range and never looked back. Ralph Lauren had 433 self-owned stores and 503 franchises in 243 locations all across the world in 2014, with total revenue of 7.45 billion dollars. The net worth of Ralph Lauren was 8 billion dollars in January 2015.

Born in a commune: Francois Pinault (15 Billion Dollars)

France's Francois Pinault, born on 21 August 1936 in Les Champs-Geraux, a commune in Brittany, had to leave his studies due to being blamed for his poor circumstances. Pinault started a timber business in Britney in 1936 and soon began trading construction materials. This marked the beginning of his famous business expansion plans; he acquired companies in losses at a bargain price.

In 1987, he got his first success when he took over a big paper manufacturing company. In 1988 he took the company public and kept on expanding the business with interest-free capital. He named the group 'Pinault-Printemps-Redoute' (P.P.R) in 1994 and turned his focus to the luxurious French group that owns Gucci, Balenciaga, Alexander McQueen, Brioni, Puma, and Volcom. Their business is spread in 120 countries. In March 2013, PPR was renamed Kering. When the annual revenue generation was 9.74 billion Euros, Forbes had estimated Penult's net worth to be 15 billion dollars.

The kid from the foster home: Leonardo Del Echo (19.1 Billion Dollars)

Echo was born in a very low-income family in Milan on 22nd May 1935. His father had passed away five minutes before his birth, and his mother could not raise him, so she left him in a foster home. He began his career as an apprentice to a tool and die-maker in Milan but decided to turn his metalworking skills to make spectacle parts. So in 1961, he moved to Agordo in the province of Belluno, which is home to most of the Italian eyewear industry. Echo started a limited partnership company by the name of "Luxottica" in 1967, and in 1971, he shut down contract manufacturing and focussed only on sales and production.

Realizing the need for vertical integration, he bought a distribution company in 1984. He also set up a subsidiary company in Germany and began his international expansion. He dealt with Armani in 1988; he got his company listed in New York in 1990 and Milan in 2000. As he continued on his acquiring spree, he added Persol and US Shoe Corporation (Lenscrafters), Ray-Ban, Sunglass Hut, Oakley, Chanel, Prada, Burberry, Versace, and Dolce, by September 2014, and Luxottica had 6000 stores across the world with total revenue of 7.31 billion Euros.

As of January 2015, Del Echo was estimated by Forbes to have a net worth of 19.1 billion dollars, making him the second richest man in Italy after the chocolate maker Michele Ferrero.

George Soros, the survivor of Nazi persecution (19.1 Billion Dollars)

Soros was born in a non-observant Jewish family in Budapest on 12th August 1930. Soros was 13 years old when Nazi Germany occupied Hungary. Jewish children were barred from attending school by the Nazis, and Soros and the other schoolchildren were made to report to the Judenrat ("Jewish Councils"). He somehow escaped and immigrated to England in 1947. He took admission to the London School of Economics as an underprivileged student and worked hard for a living. He worked as a railway porter, waiter, etc., but never gave up. He graduated in Philosophy in 1951 and got awarded with Ph.D. in 1954.

Soros went to New York in 1956 and worked as a broker merchant for F.M. Mayor. In 1959, after three years at F.M. Mayer, he moved to Wertheim & Co. as an analyst for four years. Karl Popper was Soros' tutor during this time, and they formed the Theory of Reflexivity. He served as Vice President at Arnhold and S. Bluechroeder from 1963 to 1973 and got his first opportunity to work on an offshore investment fund based on the Theory of Reflexivity in 1967. Following his success, he set up Double Eagle Hedge Fund in 1969, and In 1970, Soros set up his own company, Soros Fund Management L.L.C. The breakthrough came one week before 'Black Wednesday' (16th September 1992). His company, Quantum Fund, made a profit of 1.80 billion dollars from buying German Franks and converting them into British Pounds. **"The Man who Broke the Bank of England"** became his most famous claim to fame.

However, in 2000 Quantum Fund lost the title of the world's largest hedge fund company as the value of managed funds declined to 4 billion dollars from 10 billion dollars. But Soros was still rising and shining. In 2008, he bought shares in Lehman Brothers before they claimed insolvency, and In 2009, he acquired loans, investments, and deposits worth 160 billion dollars in only 13.9 billion dollars. In 2010, he declared his profit since 1973 to be 32 billion dollars. In 2011 his company was managing funds of 27.9 billion dollars. Soros has also earned a reputation in philanthropy with his total donations worth 8 billion dollars (1979:2011). Forbes had estimated his net worth to be 23 billion. dollars.

Li Ka-Shing, the daily labourer (19.1 Billion Dollars)

Li Ka-Shing was born in Chaozhou (Guangdong province, China) on 19 July 1928 in Chaozhou's Teochew-speaking tribe. He had to quit school when his father passed away at the age of 16. Although he got a job at a plastics trading company, he had to work 16 hours daily, and with this job, he was able to form his own company named Cheung Kong in 1950.

When the company's license renewal declined in 1958, Li had to set up his factory. This battle for survival gave him essential lessons in investment. In 1967, when people started to leave Hong Kong due to the unrest, Li saw a golden opportunity and acquired many lands as the real estate had plummeted. In the meantime, his base company had become the largest supplier of plastic flowers in Asia.

In 1972, Cheung Kong Holdings became public on the Hong Kong Stock Exchange. In 1979, he acquired Whampoa Company Limited, the part of HSBC. He was called the king of Real Estate. This deal opened the gates for him, and he gained access to various seaports in Canada (Delta port in Vancouver), China, Britain, Rotterdam, Panama, Bahamas, etc. This made him the king of the seaports. He did not stop there; through AS Watson group, a subsidiary of CK

Hutchison, he raised a chain of 7800 retail stores. This consists of Super Drug (U.K), Marionnaud (France), Kruidvat (Benelux countries), and Watsons (Asia). Bloomberg Billionaires had estimated his net worth as 31.9 billion dollars, and he was the richest man in Asia in 2014.

The boy from the hut, Harold Simmons (10 billion Dollars)

Simmons was born in a teacher family in Golden (Wood County, Texas, America) on 13th May 1931. He spent his childhood in a hut without tap water and electricity, but he succeeded in entering Texas University. After completing his graduation and post-graduation in Economics in1952, he started his career as an examiner at the Republic National Bank in Dallas. In 1960, he opened a small medical shop by the name of University Pharmacy on the campus of South Methodist University (Dallas, Texas) with $ 5000 in savings and $ 95000 in loans. He opened a chain of 100 medical stores with continuous expansion, sold them for 50 million dollars in 1973, and turned an investor. Through his experience of current banking trends, he formed a property management strategy of all debt and no equity. He started acquiring the companies through a loan from the controlling bank.

He successfully acquired a 20 percent share of the giant spacecraft manufacturer Lockheed through money raised from banks and created a storm in the stock markets when he announced the company's takeover. Even though he could not acquire Lockheed, he did become a known figure in the national arena. He kept on with his acquisition spree, and in 2006 companies Titanium Metals Corporation, the largest titanium producer in the world, multinational Chemical producer company, Valhi Incorporation, and many other public limited companies were under the umbrella of his Contran Holding Company.

Forbes had estimated his net worth to be 10 billion dollars in September 2013. On 28th September 2014, he passed away at the age of 82.

The child of an unmarried mother, Larry Ellison (56.2 Billion Dollars)

Larry Ellison was born in a densely populated immigration colony in Brooklyn, New York City, to an unwed Jewish mother. At the age of 9 months, Ellison contracted pneumonia, and his mother gave him to his aunt and uncle for adoption. His foster father did not treat him well. When his loving foster mother passed away, he quit in the second year of graduation from Illinois University Urbana Champagne and moved to Silicon Valley in northern California and did various jobs for the next eight years. In 1977, he set up a software development company with his savings of 2000 dollars.

After renaming his company several times, he named Oracle System Corporation in 1982, after its principal product Oracle Database (Object Relational Database Management System, ORDS). After that, Oracle corporation developed a series of complicated software like Enterprise Resource Planning, Customer Relation Management, and Supply Chain Management. In 2011, it was the second-largest software developer company after Microsoft.

In 2014, the net revenue generation of Oracle Corporations was 38.27 billion dollars worldwide. In 2015 Forbes estimated Larry Ellison's net worth to be 56.2 billion dollars, and he became the third richest person in America and fifth in the world.

❑

3

HOW TO FIND INFINITE TREASURE

"Mind is the Master power that moulds and makes,
And Man is Mind, and evermore he takes
The tool of Thought, and, shaping what he wills,
Brings forth a thousand joys, a thousand ills:
He thinks in secret, and it happens:
Environment is but his looking-glass."

—James Allen

Renowned British Author and Philosopher

"I have about concluded that wealth is a state of mind and that anyone can acquire a wealthy state of mind by thinking rich thoughts"

Andrew Young

Georgian-American Politician, Diplomat and Pastor

For most people, wealth remains a secret since childhood, and they are brain fed that acquiring wealth is only for fortunate ones or, in other words finding wealth is like finding a treasure hidden behind seven locked doors.

So, where is wealth? Is it in the lockers of the rich or the strong rooms of banks?

Have you ever visited these places and thought to yourself, where did such enormous money come to these banks? Instantly your answer will be from wealthy individuals. Did you again ask yourself where do these wealthy individuals get money from? The majority of us don't seek an answer to this question. Where does the money come from? Does it grow on trees or shower down from the sky for the so-called fortunate?

The treasure lies within you

In the second chapter, we have briefly dealt with the life stories of 15 billionaires. Most of them did not initially have a single penny, so how did they acquire such enormous wealth? Did you learn something from their brief stories? If not, then reread them, and if you find them less informative, read about them in detail. You will find familiar to all of them that they never compromised with the circumstances. In that sense, you can call them rare.

Now take a look around you; you will find at least one rich man even in the poorest colonies. In the village, the rich are born into wealthy families. You will also stumble upon many instances where the family used to be rich once but not anymore. This happens because the older generation worked hard to acquire wealth, but the younger generation failed to continue and spent all their hard-earned money. You might have also experienced that those who manage to keep their family wealth intact are often called miser and tightwad by the people around them and that the same people also don't fail to flatter them.

Do you realize how some people can acquire wealth while others born with fortune manage to lose it? If you cannot, then listen to the stories of these people from your elders. You will find people who have become millionaires with small businesses everywhere. To find a rich person, you don't need to go to the so-called land of fortunes like London, New York, Hong Kong, Singapore, Dubai, or Mumbai. Now concentrate on yourself and think – isn't there a treasure hidden inside you?

How could I discover this treasure? Don't answer casually without reasoning. You should keep searching till you find it. Look in your neighborhood for families where some managed to get rich while some could not. Listen to their life stories. The best source for this would be the unsuccessful person who will tell you about his kin in detail. You will realize that the successful people did not come from another planet; it's just that they had recognized the superpower within themselves, which has been gifted equally by nature to every human being.

Can you find your treasure?

Oh yes! The infinite treasure lies within you. Observe closely; it isn't visible with physical eyes but with your mental sight.

Wealth is a state of mind

People are confused about earning to their maximum capacity, and the truth is the opposite. Everybody can make enormous wealth in his life irrespective of what he is earning. To understand this, take a glance at Adolf Hitler's time; a lot of prosperous families, especially Jews, whose life turned upside down when they were locked in camps in Nazi Germany. People like Victor Frankl and Anne Frank were in extreme poverty, but still, their capacity was enormous.

Victor Frank, the survivor of the Nazi Holocaust, became a world-renowned neurologist and psychiatrist, and one of his most famous works is 'Man's Search for Meaning.'

"There is one thing that cannot take away from a man: his attitude. We who lived in concentration camps can remember the men who walked through the huts comforting others, giving away their last piece of bread. They may have been few, but they offer sufficient proof that everything can be taken from a man, but one thing can, human freedom – to choose one's attitude in any given set of circumstances, to choose one's way."

Frank chose a creative attitude to endure his pains in a concentration camp, and he also turned a man's last freedom : his attitude and picking his way to show his internal prosperity, into an asset. He used this asset in a good sense. He vindicated the universal truth that a man can battle any condition, overcome any obstacle, and keep treading his path to achieving prosperity and enormity in his life with a positive, creative attitude. This is an inspiration for those who give up when conditions get tough and spend their lives in financial insecurity and accuse their fate of it.

Anne Frank is one of the most famous girls of the same Nazi persecution. Anne's family escaped to Netherland in 1933, when the Nazis captured Germany, but in March 1940, the Nazis invaded and captured the Netherlands, and the family was trapped. In 1942, Anne's father and his family hid in the building where he used to work. They stayed in hiding for almost two years but could not escape their arrest. Eventually, Anne and her sister were put in the Bergen-Belsen concentration camp. Later in the first half of March 1945, she died (maybe due to typhus). His father was the only survivor in the family. In 1945 when the war was over, he returned to his home and gave a diary to his daughter, Anne. When this diary got published in 1947, it became legendary literature on the positive attitude of human beings. The two sisters did not let their optimist spirit die even when hiding from the Nazi soldiers. Margot Frank enrolled in a correspondence course in shorthand, while Anne Frank spent most of her time reading and writing. In her diary, Anne Frank has not only written about the incidents, but she has also penned her thoughts, ambitions, and feelings, which she did not share with anybody. Anne Frank aspired to become a journalist, and with passing years, her confidence and maturity in writing became more and more substantial. She also began to write her views on abstract subjects like faith in God, human nature, etc. What she had written on 5th April 1944, even though she was under death, is quite enough to touch the height of optimism of a man:

> ***"I want to be useful or bring enjoyment to all people, even those I've never met. I want to go on living even after my death! And that's why I'm so grateful to God for giving me this gift, which I can use to develop myself and express all that's inside me!"***

When I write, I shake off all my worries. My worries vanish, and my feelings are alive again. But the question remains: What will I ever be capable of writing so much? Will I ever become a journalist or an author?

Anne continued to write even in the concentration camp because that was her only asset. She did not let her dreams and ambitions die even when in hiding and gave the world literature, which would inspire people to struggle in difficult conditions. Anne did not waste a single moment pursuing her dream to be alive even after death. Doesn't this mean you should die to live or confront death with the open challenge of life to emerge victoriously? What was Anne's mindset that inspired her to think in the right direction?

Net Worth and Self Worth

When talking about prosperity, we must think deeply about it. As we have understood above, it is only a state of mind. Our mind is like a channel through which prosperity flows. We fail to recognize the negative thoughts and unknowingly keep mudding them, which choked the natural flow of prosperity. And we don't understand what has happened. But when we realize this asset through self-observation and understand its nature, we can harness it as we wish.

Victor Frankl found his inner channel when he was in the concentration camp. He lost everything he owned, even his shoes. As he had been stripped of all his material assets, all he was left with was his self-belief, which made him realize he was a good person.

His net worth was all the self-worth he possessed, i.e., The materials he had were stolen. Then why was he prosperous because he believed himself to be a good man, but this world measures prosperity by the value of physical objects?

So what was Frankl left with that could prove his worth? His creative attitude was impossible for the

Nazi Government and any world power to snatch. He was left with his self-worth, the power of his mind, and as its use materialized, the world started to recognize him. Material resources began to follow him, but Frankl never lets money take over his mind and kept following his mind and heart. So, why don't you too listen to your mind? Why don't you recognize yourself worth? Isn't the gold mine actually inside you?

Are you still unable to see the gold mine lying inside you? Remember that money does not determine who you are; it is merely a resource. What is most important is the self-belief that 'I am capable.' Money is just an outside element. The moment you stop comparing your capabilities regarding the money, you will feel the first doors of your inner gold mine unlocking itself. Then you will be able to enter it and also know yourself better. The inhibition will disperse, and you will feel the excitement of the next door, and then when you give one wholehearted push, you will find another door opening. You will get more courageous, and you will realize while treading on this path that you have the power to unlock infinite doors. Your inhibitions will be gone completely, and you will begin to move ahead on an endless journey of prosperity.

The first doors of prosperity and fortune will open when you are very clear in your financial goals and keep reminding yourself, "this is what I want, or my mind desires." There are many ways to achieve it, many possibilities of its incident. If nothing works, I will try something different, and if even that does not work, you are advised to try something else. This is where you should move with caution. If the desired results do not come on the first try, it doesn't mean you were wrong or failed, and it means something else. It means that you will find something that will work further in this way, and that thing is still away from your reach.

Therefore if someone tries to measure his self-worth by his net materialistic worth, the results could be disastrous. For example, a woman's parents set up a trust fund of 100 million for her, and she received 8 million every year as interest on that deposit. Now she tries to match the lifestyle of her sister, who also has the same asset. As a result, she thinks that the interest money is enough for her and starts spending the money without having an alternate source of income and goes bankrupt in a few years. At the same time, her sister had set up other businesses along with her husband and created an alternate source of income for herself. She did not care for the interest money or compare her lifestyle with others. She did not measure her worth by her property as well. She kept a balanced lifestyle without bothering about her income and property.

This habit of comparing our financial status with others is quite common, which is the cause of tension for most people. When people compare themselves with their friends, relatives, colleagues, etc., then, in fact, they are reaching, judging themselves and others by net materialistic worth and not on self-worth. You cannot determine the true self-worth of anybody till you keep measuring them by physical assets. It is a universal truth that God has created every human being with a unique talent, and until you make decisions by these talents, you won't be able to start your journey towards prosperity.

And when you start looking at yourself in the purview of your capabilities and comparing yourself with yourself, you will be able to find your shortcomings and try to amend them. Then your self-power will be awakened, and you will see yourself as a distinct and essential person. Is it not so? Even the '*Upanishads*' say: '*Aham Brahmasmi*' (I am *Brahma*), and what is *Brahma*? It is your self-realization, and a self-aware person is prosperous in the true sense. He can achieve it in any material form, but to awaken your inner power, you will have to develop the art of self-observation.

The subconscious mind, self-suggestion, and self-realization

The key to the doors of a gold mine and the root mantra of success; lies within you. And that key or mantra is known as self-realization. To attain success, a man has to realize his unique art; he must practice it and master it. In the same way, to achieve self-realization, the art that one has to develop is known-self-observation.

It is essential to understand how the human subconscious mind functions to develop the art of self-observation. Scientists from every field have acknowledged its existence, but the ultimate definition is still a matter of debate. India had announced the presence of the human subconscious mind in the Vedic period itself, and the *Vedas*, *Upanishads*, and *Puranas* present a clear description. A man becomes a spiritual person by reaching the Altus of the subconscious state of mind.

Anyway, our goal is not to go deep into spiritual reasoning, but its discussion was essential to understand the gravity and enormity of the subject. In simple words, a human brain has two parts-conscious and subconscious. You can compare the brain's structure to an iceberg, and the small portion visible above water is the conscious mind. As you cannot see the piece above without the inner portion, our habits, complexes, and personality limitations are part of the giant subconscious. In other words, whatever we think, do, or behave like is the outcome of the subconscious state. The subconscious is responsible for our overt nature and not the conditions outside.

Now the question arises: how does the subconscious, which is responsible for all our deeds, function? What is its working system? We can compare it to a computer system. The computer executes only those software programs installed on it. A man's brain also works with some software programs inherited or acquired through his parents, families, and society after birth.

Unfortunately, as we have already read, most of the software inside our minds is developed in a hostile environment; hence, our computer or subconscious keeps calculating negative results.

Unless we are aware of the law of mind, we won't understand how the software of our subconscious functions. It is not surprising if you also feel that you don't know how does this system work? Most people are unaware of this system because it starts at birth when the ability to make independent decisions has not even developed. He keeps on grasping all the suggestions from the outside world in the same manner. These suggestions become a part of the database of the hard disc of the human computer.

Modern psychiatry has proved that every human being is born with hereditary characteristics or traits, and this means that the physical and his nature will also resemble his ancestors. But a human, after appearing out of his mother's womb, is influenced mainly by the outside world, which keeps feeding his brain. . The process starts with his parents, siblings, and other family members. It keeps expanding itself from education in primary-secondary school, higher education, society, and the entire world.

The mind's data, foundation, and system development develop as a man is born. His five sensors or sense organs-eyes, nose, ears, tongue, and skin are activated, and they keep collecting different information.

Before we proceed further, it is essential to understand the sense organs, biological functions, and their impact.

Ears: every sound source sends vibrations or sound waves in the air. These waves enter our ear, flow through the ear canal, and hit the eardrum to create vibrations. Three tiny bones in the middle section of the brain channel these vibrations into the cochlea or the inner ear cavity. Sounds from different sources create a frequency of 20 Hz to 20 kHz, making different kinds of sound, and ultimately, the message is relayed to the brain. Indian classical music divides these sound waves into seven notes: *Shadaj*, *Rishabh*, *Gandhara*, *Madhyam*, *Pancham*, *Daivat*, and *Nishad*. In standard terms, these are Sa, Re, Ga, Ma, Pa, Dha, and Ni. The human brain accepts and interprets the combination of these different notes as the nine *rasas* (*Navras* or nine essences) – Amour (*Shringar*), Derision (*Hasya*), Anger (*Rowdra*), Pathos (*Karuna*), Valour (*Veera*), Wonder (*Adbhut*) Disgust (*Vibhatsa*), Fear (*Bhayanak*) and Peace (*Shanta*).

Eyes: Light rays enter our eyes through the cornea, an opening situated just in front of the eyes. The cornea refracts the light rays towards the iris so that it begins to move freely through the pupil, the center of the spherical blue structure of the eye. The iris works precisely like the shutter of a camera; it adjusts towards the frequency of lights and, with these light effects, creates images, creating a collared image using these lights. Natural light combines seven colors or frequencies – violet, indigo blue, green, yellow-orange, and red, the seven colors of a rainbow.

Nose: Actually, the smell is chemistry. These are the elements from natural and human-made sources that float in the air, and these elements tell us what is nearby. The nose has special receptors which can identify the details of these chemicals. This is because our nose responds differently to every type of smell, which creates different smell effects in our brain.

Tongue: It is a muscular hydrostat. The upper surface consists mainly of taste buds, and every taste bud has test receptor cells, which differentiate into different tastes. According to Ayurveda, these taste buds can identify six different flavors: sweet, salty, sour, bitter, and astringent: and send signals about these tastes to the brain.

Skin: this is the biggest organ of the integumentary system of the human body. It is made of several layers of ectodermic tissue, which protects the muscles, bones, and internal organs present inside the human body. It is always in direct contact with the outside environment; it acts as a shield against pathogens and the danger of excessive loss of water in the human body. The mechanical functions of the skin consist of insulation, synthesis, temperature regulation, and preservation of vitamin B and folic acid but the most vital function of the skin is to create sensations. The skin over different body parts has nerve endings that react accordingly to hot, cold, touch, pressure, vibration, and tickle and create a tactical perception in our brain for all these sensations. These touch sensations are called feelings.

A newborn's brain starts accumulating all the information, suggestions, and perceptions without any purpose because the hard disk or brain of the human form computer is empty, and there is no data fed into it. It collects information without any calculation; it keeps collecting information without knowing its use, and it keeps accumulating there. As the brain develops, it builds software programs based on its data. This is called the process of learning.

What does a child learn? Whatever he is taught or whatever he knows by himself. How is this code typed in his brain? How does software development coding in the company of parents, teachers, family members, society, and other vital national environmental conditions? Specific software programs are fed and developed by particular codes. Hence, a child grows in various aspects: feeding and playing (physical growth), reading and writing (mental), laughing, crying, sing (emotional). His essential software has already been coded into his brain until he is mature.

The hardware (body) and software (brain) of a human-computer provides a different output or decides different conditions based on the essential software program fed into his brain. In other words, how much advanced the hardware might be (how much strength a man might be); the output depends upon the software program fed into the brain; in simple terms, you can do only those things you have trained to do.

Outcomes of faulty coding: it is clear now that whatever we do is our mental programming. Therefore an erroneous program will return inaccurate results. If you have even one incorrect code, knowingly or unknowingly, it is enough to produce faulty results. Many examples of an impoverished mother could tell her child in frustration that he too can never be successful just like his father.

Although the mother utters these words in extreme frustration and anger, the child's tender mind establishes it as fact. Over time, these words might be forgotten, but they remain in the brain's huge database (hard disk). This is why incidents from your childhood are recalled in your brain seldom or often, without your command; this is the natural tendency of the human form of the computer system and is known as random access memory in computing terms.

Therefore, reading or writing is the new information you feed into your brain. How much good result-oriented software might you install in your brain? If the essential software is corrupt, i.e., negative thoughts are lying in your subconscious mind, the output will always be negative; this is so because your brain's computer accesses it through the random access memory.

This erroneous data spoils the plan whenever you make strategies and plan to get prosperous. Your efforts do not yield desired results, and you don't taste success because you don't understand the basic structure and data fed to you early in your life; hence, you don't know why your decisions prove wrong.

Reconditioning of mind through self-observation: if you sit down with tranquility and look deep into the mirror of your mind, everything will get clear. You must have heard the song by Sahir Ludhianvi, "*Tora Man Darpan*," from the movie

Kajal, but did you ever try to understand its meaning? If not, then reread this song and try to understand the words through which the writer emphasizes the universal metal configuration.

तोरा मन दर्पण कहलाये:
भले बुरे सारे कर्मों को, देखे और दिखाये, तोरा मन दर्पण कहलाये
मन ही देवता, मन ही ईश्वर, मन से बड़ा न कोय
मन उजियारा जब जब फैले, जग उजियारा होय
इस उजले दर्पण पे प्राणी, धूल न जमने पाये, तोरा मन दर्पण कहलाये
सुख की कलियाँ, दुख के कांटे, मन सबका आधार
मन से कोई बात छुपे ना, मन के नैन हज़ार
जग से चाहे भाग ले कोई, मन से भाग न पाये, तोरा मन दर्पण कहलाये

Our mind is at the root of all our actions, knowingly or unknowingly, steps we take. Spiritual contemplation has repeatedly mentioned that man has to pay for his sins committed in his previous life, or you can say that these are his inborn traits. What is the basis of all these statements? Our subconscious is under the impact of our older generations and our people in our present lives-parents, siblings, family members, teachers-schools, society, and other conditions; because our subconscious gathers information, suggestions, and thoughts from these sources naturally. It is a deadly disease, and its cure is also possible. We can recondition our faulty software programs and create new ones

How? Just like a computer software program. You can do this on your own, and you can also seek the help of an experienced psychiatrist. This process has many names-mental programming, positive thinking, self-affirmation, self-hypnosis, psycho-cybernetics, etc. But at the root of all programs is :self-observation. You can analyze the foundational software program code through self-observation when you understand your mind's laws and working system. In computing language, it is called decoding the software.

You can decode, modify, and rewrite those messages without getting stuck in the complicated process of self-observation.

The magic of self observation: Yes! Sometimes a few simple words have the power to change your life forever, i.e., they can be a specific drug for the reconditioning of your mental condition. Hence in the Indian *Sanaatan* literature (*Vedas, Upanishad, and Purana*), the term word is referred to as Brahma. Words are limitless, endless. Expression of love, bad news, and congratulatory words leave an impression on our subconscious minds.

Interestingly, these words are merely suggestions and might not be entirely grasped by our minds quickly. For instance, When your boss compliments your specific work and appreciates how you did it, he might be pleased with your work. And just congratulate you, or he might know you are going through a challenging phase, like the illness of your parents or the divorce of your husband, and is just congratulating you on cheering you up. Does your mind reject that appreciation? Don't you feel good about it? Aren't you motivated? It is also possible that you know that your boss is not happy and is just making a drama of appreciating you, but still, your mind accepts it very quickly, and you get glad. Your mind is filled with positive emotions for your boss.

There is an old saying, "Nothing succeeds like success." Is this a mere quote? No, this statement has deep psychological roots. Motivational researchers have found that the reason for the success of most motivated people in their respective fields is Self-Perception.

In a similar kind of research, two groups of 10 members were asked to answer some imaginary riddles. Seven members of the first group were declared successful despite most of them answering wrong, and seven people from the second group were declared unsuccessful. However, most of them had responded correctly, on purpose. When the task was repeated, most of the first group answered correctly, while most of the people from the second group answered wrong. This happened because when the first group members were declared successful despite answering wrong, they developed a sense of self-perception that they could be successful—the unsuccessful or negative self-perception filled in the minds of members of the second group.

Therefore self-perception is developed through self-observation. If you start believing in yourself as a successful person with strong determination, you will get good results. Self-observation is very important. Then you have to get rid of all the shortcomings one by one by self-suggestion. As the process continues, your belief will get stronger, your decisions will prove correct, and ultimately, the negative coding in your basic mental program will be erased forever. Your insight will awaken, i.e., you can see right and wrong, you will learn from your mistakes instead of shying away from them, and when this starts to happen, then believe that you are attaining self-realization. Then you will become diligent; you will look at success and failure in equilibrium, which means that precise vision will develop in you. This is what Self-realization is.

Profound philosophical descriptions have been present on this, but you don't need to go that deep in spirituality. Just recall what Shrikrisna preached to a puzzled Arjuna in Geeta; this will always inspire you towards self-realization:

कर्मण्येवाधिकारस्ते मा फलेषु कदाचन।
मा कर्मफलहेतुर्भूर्मा ते संगोऽस्त्वकर्मणि

Meaning, *"you have the right to do your duties, never in its fruit; therefore do not develop a desire for results also may you never get attracted to inaction."*

This is known as working and not knowing about it, i.e., whatever I am doing is not being done by me, but the power is controlling my subconscious mind is doing it. Then you will be able to stand witness to all your deeds. Then you will perform your jobs religiously, and your success will be predetermined. You will be able to foresee the results of all your works. When it materializes, the world will pronounce you its founder and call you successful. But this so-called success will not remain your ultimate goal. You will leave as a traveler; moving ahead will become a routine, and the achievements will be a milestone.

If you want to witness a live example of this notion, then visit any entity of a successful businessperson. You will see that even the old founders are busy with their work. In reality, they have relieved themselves from all official responsibilities, but they stay in their workplace until their last moment. Ray Kroc, the director of McDonald's, who is the foremost among the known personalities of this notion, worked until a few days before he died. As told in Geeta, this is called diligence, and anybody can become diligent.

Summary

In this chapter, you understand that the infinite treasure lies within you, and it is a state of mind which can be achieved when you develop a positive attitude inside yourself. Keep in mind that it is your attitude that no one can take from you, and nobody can stop you from moving ahead in the direction you want to.

A positive attitude in the mind awakens the self-worth of a person. Then he does not judge himself by his net worth. He stops running after it and focuses on raising his self-worth.

Self-suggestion can change mental programming.

Therefore advice yourself

- I am getting richer every day.
- I am looking for my ideal job which will provide for all my needs.
- I will rest only when I find someone who will help me realize my goal.
- I am looking for an ideal partner, and I will find him very soon.
- I am going to double my annual income.
- My capabilities are getting better, and it will help raise my income.
- I will keep on trying till my goal is achieved.
- I will not stop at the first destination. My dreams are great; I will keep moving. I am a diligent man.

❑

4

HOW TO SHED MENTAL BLOCKS

All life demands struggle. Those who have everything given to them become lazy, selfish, and insensitive to the real values of life. The very striving and hard work that we so constantly try to avoid is the major building block in the person we are today

—Pope John Paul: VI

"Don't let mental blocks control you. Set yourself free. Confront your fear and turn the mental blocks into building blocks."

—Dr Roopleen

Ophthalmologist, Motivational Counsellor & Speaker

A new structure is built by destroying the old system, and the taller the building, the deeper the foundation should be. The grandiosity, importance, and strength of the building depend upon the accurate structure of the foundation, quality of building materials, and architectural planning and execution. In the same way, to revamp your self-image and build an entirely new personality, you have to gather the courage to demolish the old structure built on a negative mindset. Then you have to develop mental architecture and draw the map for your future life monument. Building materials of a positive attitude should be stocked, and then keep treading on your path to your destination, crossing one milestone after another.

So, are you ready to change your self-image or your perception about yourself, i.e., your imagination about your life? You are willing to think like a billionaire after coming this far with this book. So, go through the summary of the previous chapters and get ready to remove your mental blockades with all the determination you can muster. This job is possible, but it is more complicated and requires more patience than expected. There is no need to get disturbed. Remember that you have to remove the mental blocks once you have determined to develop a prosperous mindset. Two kinds of blockades are prevalent on the way to success and wealth — Money is wrong and the fear of going against the family.

The fundamental importance of money

The biggest hurdle or mental block on your road to success is the thought that money is a bad thing, and if you move ahead on this path, you are walking a dirt road. This also is an erroneous software program coded in our subconscious mind. According to people accustomed to living an impoverished life, the desire to become rich is an infectious thought. Those who desire to get rich are dishonest, cunning, brainless, capitalist, shameless, impolite, and materialist.

This thought remains the old moralist mindset of those who have embraced their failure. Time has changed, but these bits of medieval philosophy are still engraved in them. Are these people moralists, or are they faking it? Take a close look at them, and you will realize that these people have made the saying 'grapes are sour' a way to live their lives. When they see someone trying to reach the grapes, they pronounce the efforts as waste by reiterating that grapes are sour, without a taste, or the lust for the grapes while calling them spoiled. In reality, those who lecture do not aspire for money, actually lust for it. However, they only desire and do not do anything to achieve it. These phony people know the importance of money but are reluctant to work hard to achieve it. And this is why they have been unsuccessful so far. Behind this reluctance are the remains of their prejudice in their subconscious.

Another common hurdle on the road to wealth is the family background and the fear of going against your upbringing. Although not all suffer from this disease, the fear of going against your family's beliefs makes the road to success look dangerous and slippery. As we have read in the second chapter, frustrations and restrictions did not become a hurdle in their path; they acted as a catalyst. In chemistry, a catalyst is a substance that either does not take part in a chemical reaction but increases or decreases the speed of the process. Hence, the family background insults and frustrations can increase your speed if you look at them with a positive mindset. This happened to those billionaires who broke their family's shackles and attained the heights that became a benchmark for others.

The question that arises at this point is, why can't we shed our inhibitions? People who have become billionaires from low-income families have proven that poverty can be ended. And those who believe that their poor economic background will not let them walk the road to success have a severe mental illness and need a cure. How much harsh these words might seem, it is the only truth. Those who can't contemplate their better future and who don't try to realize and rectify their negative attitude are mentally ill and need the help of a psychiatrist.

Remember that no condition or constraints are so tricky or unachievable that a human mind can't solve them. Those who realize and understand the capabilities of their mind can not only become successful but can also shape their present and future as they wish through their aspirations, ambitions, and desires. Those aware of the fundamental laws and implementing them in their lives can become anything :yes, anything, nothing can stop them. The condition will submit to them and become their slave; they will dictate terms, becoming the king, a kingmaker, masters of their wish. Here, we tell you about these fundamental principles that will lead you to prosperity.

The actual importance of money

If somebody's mind is prejudiced with the thought that money is filthy and he is reluctant to rise above his family's expectations, then it is shameful, but there are no words to condemn this thought. To pronounce any man who has monetary ambitions as selfish and capitalist is a misguided thought. We are not talking about the wealth that someone has inherited or won in a lottery or gambling, nor are we talking about the wealth accumulated by indulging in anti-national activities or illegal businesses. But what about someone who has acquired wealth through his hard work, dedication, and honesty? This is the result of honest hard work. Should that man be praised or condemned?

Let us discuss this point in more detail. When an entrepreneur acquires great wealth, he does not do it alone. Neither is he the only one who benefits from it. No one can earn that much alone. He has to the enterprise for it, i.e., he has to develop a structure of his business for proper functioning, in which he takes services of professionals. This means for his success; an entrepreneur employs hundreds, thousands of people based on their skills, i.e., he allows them to make money. So is this not a social service of the entrepreneur.

Maximum people don't consider this a social service. Why? Because people believe that top entrepreneurs expand their businesses to achieve their own goals or raise their income and ensure their success trap skilled people and exploit them are in the majority. It could be valid to some extent, but is it too difficult to find an example in present times where a person or business entity has risen to a great height by exploiting its employees? Even if we consider small entities, then no one can become successful unless he gains the confidence of his employees. Then why criticize becoming rich yourself and those who allow others to become rich. Are the employees of a bankrupt entrepreneur ready to work for them, even though they have made their living from him for a long time? Why?

This is because a bankrupt entrepreneur has no enterprise left where he can allow others. When you look at this way, you will understand why an entrepreneur earns more than the employees do. The simple explanation is that an entrepreneur is more skilled than his employees, so he makes more, and his income is due to his skills and talents. Then why envy the wealth of billionaires?

Look at yourself. You will realize how deep the water beneath you is. If you are capable, then some entrepreneur has entrapped you so that you don't earn more. You will find various examples where an employee has left his employer far behind. Why? Because while working for his employer, the employee develops his artistry and entrepreneurship skills. This means that a worker can also become an entrepreneur; an employee can become an employer.

Contrary to this, those who drift from the path go bankrupt. Hence, billionaires entrepreneurs also indulge in social service, and they deserve to be respected. Those who frown upon these billionaires need to ask themselves – Can I be an entrepreneur?

Yes! Entrepreneurship is the only way to become rich. The day you decide to become rich and start on that path, you will benefit only from the experience of successful entrepreneurs. Hence those who envy the rich can never be rich because a positive attitude is necessary for successful entrepreneurship. We have mentioned the life story of the top ten billionaires in world history, most of whom came from low-income families. Is it that only they or their family become rich?

Consider Henry Ford, for example. He earned billions of dollars, and what did he give in return to the world. Through his patience, talent, and determination, ordinary mechanics gave the world the motor vehicle (car). Can you imagine a world without cars today? Today, Ford Motor Company employs more than 181 thousand people. When Ford adopted the assembly line manufacturing system, he faced a backlash for turning humans into mechanical components. But that experiment gave a new direction to the motor industry. Even though he was called pinchpenny jokingly, he tried to explain the relevance of money in his life. Somebody once asked him: "What if your entire business shuts down? What will you do then?" without blinking. He answered, "I will look for some other basic human necessity, try to deliver cheaper and better services, and become a billionaire again in five years. "

Yes! The art of identifying the basic human needs and providing them in a better and cheaper way is called entrepreneurship, making people rich. Walt Disney distributed joy in the lives of millions of kids and made money. Thomas Watson built the I.B.M computer from his talent and made many people's lives better and more convenient. Conrad Hilton presented better comfort and facilities to travelers worldwide with his chain of hotels and made himself rich through it. This list is quite long. Think for a while, who are the people behind all the world's progress? Of course, it is the result of entrepreneurs' labor and hard work worldwide. Ask those who envy the rich — have they ever done anything for anybody?

The fortune path of the wealthiest people in history

Now let us tell you about the wealthiest people of all time. This assessment order is according to Therichest.com (8th April 2014). In these short stories, you will find examples of entrepreneurship, the fundamental mantra to become rich. You will also learn that wealth can be a fortune for anybody, provided he wants to become rich and is ready to do anything. You can compare these rich people to the sea divers who risk their lives to find rare pearls.

> **"Those who seek will find, but one needs to dive deep; he who is scared of getting drowned will stay sitting on the shore."**

Now, let us learn about the dynamic entrepreneurs who were so determined that even misfortune surrendered before them and made their entry into the wealthiest list.

John Jacob Astor (121 Billion Dollars)

John Jacob Astor (July 17, 1763 – March 29, 1848) was a German:American businessperson, merchant, real estate mogul, and investor. He was the first multi-millionaire in America. Johann started his professional career as his father's assistant in his diary. In 1779, at the age of 16, he moved to London to join his brother George in working for a musical instrument manufacturer; while he was there, he learned English and migrated to America at 21. And opened a butcher shop along with his younger brother in New York and then started trading in fur with Native Americans. After creating his monopoly there, he built a vast empire of immovable assets. His net market worth at the time of his death was 121 billion dollars in 2014.

Cornelius Vanderbilt (185 Billion Dollars)

Cornelius Vanderbilt (27th May 1974 to 4th January 1877) was born in a Dutch American family. He began working on his father's ferry in New York Harbour, quitting school at 11. At 16, Vanderbilt borrowed $100 from his mother and started his ferry service. Later he expanded his business to steamer service and became the emperor of the shipping and railway industry. His inflated worth in April 2014 at the time of his death was 185 billion dollars.

Henry Ford (188 Billion Dollars)

Henry Ford (30th July 1863 to 7th April 1947) was born in an Irish farming family. At 16, he started his professional career as a trainee machinist against his father's wish. After working hard for almost 12 years, he became an engineer in 1891. He quit his job as a chief engineer in 1893 and started to work on gasoline-based engines, and in 1896 he made ethanol fuelled four-wheeled motor vehicles. With ongoing experiments and struggle, he formed the Ford Company in 1903. In 1906 he presented the T-car, developed the assembly line manufacturing system, and created history in automobile manufacturing. The inflated value of his property at the time of his death was 188 billion dollars in April 2014.

Muammar Gaddafi (200 Billion Dollars)

Muammar Gaddafi (1942 to 23rd August 2011) was born in a tribal shepherd family in the deserts of western Libya. He had studied until the 6th standard in a mosque 20 miles away from his home. He was pestered and called 'Bedouin.' But instead of giving up, he continued to fight for the rights of the Bedouin students and entered Libya University (Benghazi). He quit his study of history midway to join the army. He kept on achieving higher ranks in the military to become the chairperson of the Revolutionary Command Council and indirectly took governance into his control. He nationalized the oil industry alongside other economic reforms, announced the Great Socialist People's Libyan Arab Jamahiriya in 1977, and ruled as the brotherly leader until 2011. In the meantime, his personal property kept on rising. The inflated value of his properties at his death was 200 billion dollars in April 2014.

William-I (230 Billion Dollars)

William-I (9th September 1028 to 1087), also known as William the Conqueror, was the illegitimate son of the Duke of Normandy and his mistress, a tanner's daughter. Robert had no heir from his wife; still, Robert had to struggle to sit on the throne because of his illegitimacy and tender age of 8. He conquered his neighboring kingdoms, expanded his empire and property, and finally became the first Norman king of England. The inflated value of his property in April 2014 at the time of his death was 230 billion dollars. However, his property was divided into his predecessors subsequently.

Osman Ali Khan, Asaf Jah-VII (240 Billion Dollars)

Osman Ali Khan Siddiqui Bahadur, Asaf Jah :VII (6th April 1886 to 24th February 1967) was born in the old palace in the princely state of Hyderabad (present Telangana). He became the Nizam of Hyderabad after his father's death in 1911, the biggest province of pre-independent India. The area covered 86,000 square feet. His empire spanned 2,233,000 square miles, an area almost as large as the United Kingdom today, and his wealth was derived from mining royalties, not land revenue. In the late 19th century, British India was the only world supplier of diamonds.

After the merger of Hyderabad in India in 1948, Osman Ali remained the nominal Nizam until he died in 1967. The lands that stayed with him after the acquisition by the government became a serious legal battle amongst his 149 children from 7 wives and 42 concubines.

Andrew Carnegie (320 Billion Dollars)

Andrew Carnegie (25th November 1835 to 11th August 1919) was born in a typical weaver's cottage. Due to nationwide starvation and struggling to make ends meet, his family moved to Allegheny (Pennsylvania, America) for the prospect of a better life. Carnegie's first job in 1848 was as a bobbin boy, changing spools of thread in a cotton mill. He worked 12 hours a day, six days a week, in a Pittsburgh cotton factory. His starting wage was dollars 1.20 per week. Two years later, he began working as a telegraph messenger and doubled his income to 2.50 Dollars with his hard work. In 1853, he became a telegraph operator in

Pennsylvania Railroad Company, and his weekly pay became 4 dollars. Learning all the business strategies, he kept on earning promotions and ultimately became the superintendent of the Pittsburgh division. In 1964, he invested 40,000 dollars in Real Estate. A year later, he made a profit of 100,000 dollars. He set up a steel rolling mill and raised his business manifold with this capital. During his last years, he donated 90 percent of his properties, worth 350 Million dollars (4.76 Billion in 2015 dollars), to local libraries, world peace, education, scientific research, and many other philanthropic works. Still, his net worth at the time of his death in 1919 was 320 billion dollars in 2014.

Rothschild Family (350 Billion Dollars)

Mayer Amschel Rothschild (23rd February 1744 to 19th September 1812) was born in a Jewish ghetto of Frankfurt am Main, Holy Roman Empire. His family was in the business of goods trading and currency exchange. Before he returned to his family's business, Rothschild and his elder brother worked as an apprenticeship under Jacob Wolf Oppenheimer, a director of a Jewish bank in Hanover. He became a dealer in rare coins and won the patronage of Crown Prince Wilhelm of Hesse, following which he expanded his business to include some princely patrons. By the early years of the 19th century, Rothschild had consolidated his position as principal international banker to Wilhelm and began to issue his international loans. Long before that, he had sent his third son to become a garment merchant, who established the City of London Bank in 1804 as a neutralized citizen. In 1806, Napoleon invaded Hesse, and Wilhelm was forced into exile in the Dutch of Holstein, but Rothschild was able to continue as his banker. In 1810, Mayer entered into a formal partnership agreement with his sons, thus establishing the banking dynasty. One of his sons was sent to Paris in 1811, enhancing the family's ability to operate across Europe. The Rothschild family became the most fortunate family of the 19th century. Although that stature is no longer there, the inflated value of the family was 350 billion dollars in 2014.

John D. Rockefeller (400 Billion Dollars)

John Davison Rockefeller (1839– 23rd May 1937) was the second of six children and the eldest son born to a salesperson in Richford, New York. At the age of 16, in 1855, he started working as a bookkeeper. In 1859, Rockefeller went into the produce commission business with a partner. He rose swiftly and became a wholesale trader of food grains. In 1963, he established his first oil refinery, and in 1970 he established Standard Oil. Gradually he established a monopoly over the oil business in entire America through horizontal integration. He was the first man in America to have a net worth of 1 billion dollars. The estimated inflated value of his property at the time of his death in 1937 was 400 Billion dollars.

Mansa Musa First (410 Billion Dollars)

The tenth *Mansa* (emperor) of the Kieta dynasty, the Mali kingdom ruled for 25 years and accumulated infinite treasure through gold and salt mining, almost half of the total world supply. However, the stats are not very assertive, and it's a matter of debate. Still, the inflation adjustment of his property was 410 billion dollars in 2014.

Self-imagination of being rich already

Calm your mind and tell yourself, "I am rich already." Repeat it. Do you feel something strange? If yes, then you are seriously thinking about strategies to become rich. If the answer is no, you need to reread the earlier chapters. We have reached that stage in our discussion where a complete strategy map has formed in your mind. After this stage, only the words 'I can be rich will not work. The complete diagram of your determination to become wealthy should be clear in your mind. If it is not so, the traces of metal blocks are still present in your mind. You are still afraid of the risk. Now you must jolt away this inhibition and believe that you are rich already.

This is known as the art of self-imaging. You won't be able to imagine your true self until the software of your subconscious mind is neutral. That means you have still not started self-evaluation. It is like the self-immolation of your older, petrified self. Yes! Repeat to yourself, 'you can't go to heaven unless you die.' Immolate all your mental blocks because they have no existence. It is only an image of your inhibitions. Light the lamp of your mind, and you will see all your faults and then give one hard stroke of courage and self-confidence. How will entrepreneurship be worshipped? How will goddess Lakshmi be called on? The beginning of the auspicious start happens in the temple of your mind.

Repeat to yourself : 'I am already rich'. Now you can visualize whether you can be rich or not. Do you feel that you have not made any strong initiative? If yes, then what are you can do naturally? How could you see your faults if you have not yet done self-reflection or introspection? If you can see them now, then make a list of them and try to remove them every day. There is no formula for it, which you can learn, and your mindset begins to reform. You and only your efforts can do it. This book, and for that matter, any book, can help you only in positive thinking. After all, only you will have to do this to get rid of your suspicions. Self-imaging will work miracles in this job.

Unless you can see what you can become, how will you work to become that? Everybody has their way of becoming successful. You will have to find your own. Don't be perturbed if the path is not visible. This mind game is a bit complex. Sit quietly, just like that, and think, 'I am already rich. Yes, sir, our subconscious is very rich. Many unused secrets are lying in there. First, you need to see yourself indifferent to your past, birth, parents, siblings, family members, relatives, school, teacher, and society. This can be done only when you stop thinking about the future. Don't give any command to your brain. Become your observer. Look at the images it shows, and you will realize that you don't have any past or future in reality. You exist only in the present. You don't know what will happen a few years from now. You are not even aware of what happened a few moments ago. Your inhibitions will shed away, and once that happens, you can visualize all those things you can become. If you think too far, you will get confused. Concentrate only on the next move.

You know what you can do, so just do them without stopping, without getting tired, solid determination.

As soon as you take your first step forward, the second step will become apparent, and then keep moving, don't stop until you have achieved your goal. You should know that you won't even notice when you reached your target and are now focusing on the next step. This is what we call 'the journey to find yourself; material wealth is just a tiny portion of this journey. The bigger goal is to reach nearer to your inner self, inside you. Try to do a little self-imaging; everything will become clear itself. You will find that you were already rich, and when it becomes visible, your efforts will automatically materialize themselves. This is what happened to all the historic billionaires, and so why can't it happen to us?

Plant positive thoughts in your mind

We all know that as you sow, so shall you reap. While trying to become rich, plant the seeds of positivity in your mind. In everyday life, our thoughts are the reason for our character and deeds, just like the rule of cause and effect prevails in the physical world and just like there is a reaction for every action. This means that you build your life by the prevalent thoughts in your mind, like thoughts and events.

We will have to analyze our thoughts very minutely. We have to restrict ourselves to think only in positive ways, and if we believe it, we can do it.

If you are constantly giving your financial troubles a place in your mind and can't stop repeating that you can be bankrupt, then it means you have established the fact in your mind that you can become bankrupt long before you become one, and then it is sure to happen. You will become bankrupt. You have seen it first, and the world will see it later.

Let it be clear that the idea is not to encourage any reckless thought or act. A very fine line separates hope and pretense, foresight and morale. We don't intend to encourage you to adopt the policy of an ostrich, which hides its head in the sand when trouble comes, or like a pigeon that shuts its eyes when it sees a cat. Every business and entrepreneurship has problems and difficulties. As discussed in this or the other chapter, every billionaire or several other wealthy people had made one thing sure – that difficulties could never defeat them.

Indeed, the road to success has thorns, and everybody has to walk over them to become successful; those who crossed it find more thorns laid in their way; they have come over new difficulties. They have to clear their path. Treading this path, they have to bleed, but they never give up; they dress their wounds, get new shoes, find new ways to clear the roads, and keep moving forward. Success is far for those who get afraid. Yes, of course, others might see them as failing in their efforts, but every failure is an experience. They try another time with more preparation and keep repeating this process until the path is clear and they march forward. Oh yes! Every battle is an experience for a warrior, and the subsequent struggle looks more accessible than the previous one, and thus they reach closer to victory. You cannot succeed unless you fail, and you can be successful only when you learn from your past mistakes and keep trying.

As an entrepreneur keeps moving forward on the road to success, his experiences sharpen his foresight in his business, and then he can look through opportunities in the industry. For this, he has to live and die with his dreams. You heard it right! Live and die, both. To keep your dream alive and the determination to even die to fulfill it is what it means to live and die with your dream.

I mention Kabir's verse: "***Kabira khada bazaar main liye lukhati haath, Jo ghar jare Apna, chale hamare saath.***" In these lines, the great mystic poet says to burn down the house of your ignorance to achieve the spiritual goal of life (God). I don't want to go deep into this spiritual philosophy but intend to make it very clear that you have to prepare for the battle, overcome your shortcomings to achieve the goals in your life, and then your victory is assured. You will see your success before others see you fighting on the battlefield. Fighting is only your duty, and its fruit will be visible to you.

Yes! It is no secret or magic which you or anybody else cannot learn. It is the imagination power of successful people which allows them to see through their goals, meaning they can make correct estimations of their path and the difficulties that lie ahead. Therefore their dreams are realized automatically like magic. But this power does not come by itself. One has to put in hard work with lots of determination and work on new strategies to master the art. Whoever follows this will awaken his imagination power and will be able to look through his goals.

What does the imagination power of the mind give? Ideas, yes! The ideas distinguish an individual from the crowd. Others won't be able to see these ideas unless presented to the world in their material form. Before that, it is visible only to the person who holds these ideas. Since he is aware of his ideas' competitive and material abilities through his experience, he can best analyze the results before they materialize. Hence the opinion 'ideas rule the world' prevails. This is the reason why we are stressing the point that you should fill your mind with positive, prosperous, and successful thoughts. Every good idea will awaken the energy channels within you, and the secret theory of attractive personality will work like magic. Things, which resemble your thoughts, will be attracted to you and will cause the incident of similar events, and you will get desired results.

This implies that once you do self-imaging and start filling your mind with subsidiary thoughts in your mind, the power to attract your desired results will awaken within you. The more you boost these thoughts, the more accurate the results will be. You should also be careful that the results will be likewise if you fill yourself with negative thoughts. Hence it would help if you filled your mind with the positive reviews of your goals, which will replace all the negative thoughts in your mind, and as the process moves forward, the cloud of positivity will get denser.

Chase your dreams with a strong will

You must have heard the down to earth, self-satisfied people who have surrendered before the difficulties and adverse circumstances :'

जाहि विधि राखे राम ताहि विधि रहिये.'

This is profound spiritual philosophy preached by Shri Krishna to Arjuna to perform his duties without thinking about the results. However, people carved the definition; one should leave everything to God, cannot challenge fate, and should surrender before the circumstances and don't dare to challenge the difficulties lying ahead of you. It is necessary to avoid the company of such apathetic people and protect yourself from their worthless advice. They can carve out the point of idlers even in thoughts of high morale.

Arjun also advocated this idea and told Shri Krishna battle was not a good option. And then Krisha took his grand form and imparted the divine knowledge to Arjun.

So, do you need to visualize the great form? Look closely at your inner self, and you can see the great possibilities and your real dreams. But you will have to work hard continuously without caring about the result, just like Arjuna had to keep his oath and fulfill his promise. This is known as chasing your dreams. This is what you were born to do. This was your true purpose, and you are afraid to pursue this very purpose, to perform your duty. Try to walk on this path of your mind. You will start enjoying and worshipping your work, and then your goals won't be only your results.

Daydreaming won't work. Your dreams won't fulfill themselves by sitting idle, be practical and self-satisfied. It would help if you chased your dreams with such intense passion that you are even willing to die. Half-hearted efforts will never materialize and turn into pessimistic false evidence and excuses for not putting more effort. Then you will say that I did try very hard but could not succeed. Take a peek inside your mind; did you put in all the efforts? You will realize that you did not do so. To fulfill your dreams, you will have to make efforts with solid determination and vouch that you shall not rest until you flourish.

Unfortunately, our education system also tries to make us more pragmatic than required and imparts the counter-narrative in our minds. This so-called practical education does not help in understanding the immense capabilities of our subconscious mind but tries to put the veil of narratives between ourselves and the essential attitude of our mind. Our education system does enhance our reasoning information, but it also makes our subconscious mind, spiritual mind, and self-confidence dormant by reasoning. This is why we don't heed the advice and intuitions of our subconscious mind and negate them as impractical views. The right side of the brain tries to put in real dreams through its natural knowledge and imagination. Unless you can see these dreams, called self-projections, there is no chance of them being realized.

It means that you can self-project whatever thoughts you fill in your mind, whatever you imagine, and once you make efforts to fulfill them, your success is guaranteed. Everybody does self-projection in solace, whether a businessperson, entrepreneur, artist, painter, or scientist. In spiritual terms, this is known as meditation. It is possible with some effort, and then you can also learn the art of self-projection. In straight words, you should listen to your inner voice. In spiritual terms, this is easy to attain internal knowledge, known as insight or enlightenment. So when you dream of thick spontaneously strategizing accordingly and overcoming all your shortcomings with all dedication and determination, your path is clear, and victory is yours.

Summary

- **Identify your mental blocks regarding wealth and success:** look for your correlation and opportunities with wealth. Please make a list of them, negative or positive. Analyze them and think about presumptions that make you feel that way. Then try to change the reasons behind the negative thoughts.
- **Look closely at your thoughts:** focus on your virtues. Call for the immenseness of maximizing prosperity and success in your life and do this every day. Don't be afraid of this self-observation. In the beginning, many shortcomings will come out; try to remove them in natural ways.

- **Extract an image of yourself that you are already wealthy:** replace your negative thoughts with positive thoughts. The more positive thoughts are in your mind, the more precise image to see your possibilities realize your true capabilities.
- **Chase your dreams with passion:** dreaming is not enough; you must chase it with all your power. In the beginning, this race will look complex, the road will seem very long, but as you keep progressing on this road, your destination will seem nearer. You will go on crossing them; the journey will become your destination, and success will become your birthright.

❑

5

HOW TO MASTER THE SKILL OF DECISION MAKING

"When I look at acting careers that I really admire, I see that it's been a precise decision-making process for these people. They make decisions based on what they love, and they do only the things that they are passionate about. They play only characters that they can't stop thinking about."

—Taylor Alison Swift

American pop star and singer

"Inability to make decisions is one of the principal reasons executives fail. Deficiency in decision-making ranks much higher than lack of specific knowledge or technical know-how as an indicator of leadership failure."

—John C Maxwell

American author, speaker and padre

We have learned that it is essential to believe in your actions. The fourth wealthiest man in world history, Andrew Carnegie, had once asked Napoleon Hill, a renowned self-help author, to do extensive research and survey to find the secret formula for the success of the wealthy people. Hill presented the results of this research in one word : Belief, which means that man can accomplish anything that he believes in.

Does the question arise whether we can succeed only by believing in ourselves? How do you know the job or thought you believe in is accurate? On what grounds do you think whatever you are yearning for and making all the efforts is not a fatal mistake? Every day we come across news about industrialists and people in the business whose decisions had brought an existential crisis. Even the most experienced person can make the wrong decision, bringing down all the name and wealth they had acquired.

Precise decision making is as essential as self-belief

The decisions in life can be so powerful that they can demolish the castle of your success. It proves that the results can be astonishing if your choices are correct. Yes indeed! Even one right decision is so powerful that it can propel you to the highest point of success. We often come across examples of such decisions, which are fatal, but the results are astonishing and propel the decision-maker to the peak of success. Hence right choices in life are as important as beliefs.

Now, the actual point is how to learn the art of correct decision-making and self-belief? How can we escape from mistakes when even legends couldn't do so? If this thought comes to your mind, then it's pretty natural. Yes, anybody can make a mistake, even we. We all make mistakes, but we can learn the art of making the correct decision. This art can minimize the chances of making the wrong decision, and then the adverse effects can be confined. The art of keeping the negative impact of your decision in control is known as a calculated risk, and in modern business management terms, it is called risk management.

Remember that it is not some unique art that only a few distinct elites can learn. Any commoner can understand it. But those who master it do not remain common anymore; they become extraordinary. Their decisions start becoming right, and the impact on their life and business takes a U-turn. Their velocity of success does not slow down. Such people are always getting ready to pay for the losses. Hence, when failures happen, they are prepared to face them even after all the preparations.

This is a hard truth that we can't avoid decision-making. We have to make decisions whether we like it or not. Whatever the context is – to continue with your job, look for new opportunities, keep supporting any project, or make further investments in every topic. We make correct decisions, and we have to make decisions to move forward in life. It is pretty clear that once we have made up our minds to become rich, we have to make correct and accurate decisions, or else all the labor put in so far would go in vain. But since we have decided to become rich, we will make the right decision and keep the results in our control through calculated risk.

The art through which we can distinguish the thoughts that bring better prospects from all the spontaneous ideas coming into our mind, or you can develop new thoughts, will bring you immense success. This art will ensure the thoughts that will enable our success, and we should believe in them.

So how do we start, and how do we find the thoughts that will ensure our success? The answer is simple, and the universal laws are also applicable here. Yes, indeed, the common or the prevailing thoughts in the maximum population will seldom bring you success, and the proof of this is that if the ideologue of success is so simple and known to all, then why are most the people not wealthy?

You can choose any field. Work has been going on in them for thousands of years, but there are mostly service members, few executives, and fewer entrepreneurs. Even amongst the entrepreneurs, most reach the lower level of success; some get the middle, while very few attain the topmost point of success. Why do most people fail in achieving the top position despite the same profession and industry? Why don't they become equally rich although they all have equal knowledge of the job and industry? They even have many inspirations for success in front of them. When you look at the people on the last, mid, and topmost step of the ladder, it will become apparent why only a few manage to reach the top. Only a few are masters in analyzing and distinguishing the ideas of better possibilities. They could see through the obstacles lying in their way; they mustered the courage to overcome this obstacle, showed the capabilities to recognize the resources necessary to ensure their success, and continued on their path with strong determination, patience, and dedication.

Yes! Achieving success in any field is like walking a tightrope. One wrong move is not necessarily fatal but can be a blowback. We will have to learn the art of correct decision-making. We must say yes only at the opportune moment; otherwise, we should say no and postpone all the business deals. What is encouraging here is that every wealthy person has acknowledged this art was not inborn, but they had realized its importance at the outset of their professional life. They not only nurtured this art but also continuously polished it through regular practice. This way, they did not even know when they had mastered this art. This suggests that if someone is enthusiastic enough and puts in time and energy, he can master this unique art of making the right decision.

Suppose you can look at the possibilities in something where others can only find impossibilities. In that case, you will be able to make the right decisions and will leave before everybody sees it. This is why people often mistake rejecting the opportunities when they come knocking at their doors. Therefore you must ignore the talks of those who criticize your efforts or keep throwing the pebbles of comments in your way. What you should keep in mind at this point is that these critics can be people around you or the specialists from that field who will try to give logical explanations. Even in these circumstances, you should remain determined, see-through, and remove all the obstacles using your spontaneous thoughts. These spontaneous thoughts will enhance your decision-making and enable you to differentiate between feasible and infeasible. Then you can find the road to the gold mines while the others won't be able to see.

Mark Hume McCormack, the founder of International Management Group (IMG), an organization dealing with media management of sports and communication, presents an interesting example of the failure of infeasible planning in his book 'What they don't teach you in Harvard Business School':

A dog food manufacturing company was organizing its annual sales conference. During the convention, the company's chairperson listened carefully to the power point presentation on plans to bring revolutionary growth in sales given by the company's advertising director. Finally, it was the chairperson's turn to speak.

He started speaking, "For the past few days; we have listened to the different heads of the divisions who presented brilliant plans for the coming year. Now we are heading to a conclusion; I have only one question. If we have the best advertisements, marketing, and sales team, why do we sell less dog food than those in this business?"

There was a stunned silence in the room. Ultimately, as it has always happened, a meek voice from the back answered, 'because the dogs hate it.'

Even the best marketing or advertising won't help an inferior product or service that doesn't fill the need. How do we know if our plan is viable or not? You will find it with the help of your intuition, which we often neglect in our course of preparation. Just remember, when the Wright brothers made the airplane, many scientific studies of that time had suggested that no such thing, which is heavier than air, could fly.

The story of Soichiro Honda also presents a lively example of decision making on intuition in his autobiography:

When I started manufacturing motorcycles, many doomsayers (prophets of the judgment day), who were also good friends, came to discourage me. Why don't you set up a garage? You will make loads of money. There are so many cars in the country that need repair, and I did not heed that pessimistic advice. I started Honda Motor Company alongside my research laboratory, which has spread worldwide.

Oh Yes! Soichiro Honda, the weird kind of optimist, had seen through the viability of his project with his intuition, known as gut sense. While the others were unable to see it and tried to discourage him, he was strongly determined by his decision and proved it right through his determination and dedication. He writes further:

We were a group of impoverished but hard-working people who were very cautious about the risk we had taken with our small investment of 1 million yen. We hoped to bring an industrial sector out of the depression when the national industry was in shatters. We were taking a vacuous risk of manufacturing motorcycles when people were so poor that they could not afford to buy petrol. When their economic conditions improved, they would have certainly wanted to buy cars. We were drifting even in the eyes of the most optimistic economic forecast.

Ray Kroc had the same experience. The possibilities in McDonald's fast-food restaurants, which were visible to Ray, were invisible to its founder brothers.

This happened when the McDonald brothers had laid the foundation and worked hard to make it successful at some level. But they got bored of their beyond par success, and they decided to live the rest of their lives in comfort, and their working capabilities started to slow down.

On the other hand, 52-year-old Ray was full of energy and enthusiasm. He had the intuition to make correct decisions and look through the possibilities. He possessed the art of implementation and the quality of resource and institution building. As a result, the world sees Ray Kroc as an inspiration while feeling sorry for the McDonald brothers.

Now let us learn from the founder of the excellent retail corporation Wal-Mart, Sam Walton, how he recognized the opportunities and made the right decisions. In his autobiography, 'Made in America,' Walton writes:

"Most of our opportunities came out of necessities. Since we had started with minimal capital and financial securities, things that we were forced to do helped us grow as a company."

This shows that Sam Walton learned from his helplessness and took decisions out of compulsion; his intuition did not let him make such mistakes that could prove fatal, and gradually he spread all over the world.

The art to see problems as opportunities

It is clear now that people who can see opportunities in what others see as the problem can make the right decisions and become successful. This is the secret mantra of the art of making the right decisions and success. This theory applies to inventions or large-scale industries and small businesses and every effort we make in our lives.

How often have you seen a person raising fingers on his projects that seem impossible? How often have you decided to do the unthinkable when the opposite was relevant and nothing seemed achievable? We quit dreaming due to so-called logical reasons and a lack of self-confidence, or we console ourselves that it would not be possible. This problem is directly linked to self-observation. The better you can self-observe or the better you can map yourself, or the more confidence you have in yourself, the more you will be able to see the opportunities around you, and then you will be able to take more risks to work on those opportunities. How can we work on something we can't see, and what shall we gain when we don't work?

The truth is that unrealized projects are neither feasible nor infeasible at conception. They are mere projects which could be successful or unsuccessful; because the result of any project depends upon the quality and amount of energy invested in it. These projects you understand only when you are capable of self-observation; you only know your capabilities and pump in all your energy. You will realize that your abilities were much more than anticipated, and the results will also be much better than expected. Yes indeed! You only had not estimated your possibilities in their actual capacity. Still, you have not realized the secret force within you, the true power of your subconscious mind.

Estimating the obstacles from an exaggerated perspective is a prevalent human tendency, which hinders the accurate calculation of the possibilities of your plans. Hence, those who know more are more prone to commit mistakes. Only collecting data about the goal is insufficient because information only exaggerates the hindrances. This is the same as saying that when most people could not succeed, how could you be successful? But here lies the opportunity, which only the successful can see. Isn't it interesting that we tend to get afraid based on the experience of many unsuccessful people instead of taking inspiration from a few successful people and are unable to muster the courage to test our true potential?

Remember that trying your infinite capabilities does not mean overlooking the possible hindrances when under stress. The intention here is to neutral assess your abilities without getting alarmed by failures that others have faced. When you do so, you will be able to view the obstacles and the opportunities and your capabilities to achieve them. Then, the blocks won't dismay you; instead, they will encourage you to rectify your mistakes to overcome them. As you keep on enhancing your skills, you will be able to see more opportunities in your plan. When you attain the necessary skills, your project will take its great form, and you will have become so exuberant by then that it will start materializing on its own and bring unexpected results. This is how you can analyze a project better and more efficiently, which is the driving force of every successful person. Hence it is said that win over yourself, and your success is assured.

If a project has opportunities, there are obstacles as well. Let us ponder, why do a few barriers restrict our pursuit of innumerable opportunities? You will realize that you could not see the opportunities because the obstacles had blocked your view, and this is the shortcoming that should be earmarked at first. Unless we do not get rid of this flaw, we cannot make a precise judgment, and hence we cannot make the right decision. If we cannot make the right decision, the results will also be likewise. This is what happens to unsuccessful people. Their plans fail one after another due to wrong choices, their passion dies down, and they give up. But we cannot let ourselves be entrapped in this psychological trap; we must march forward on the road to prosperity and success with strong determination. Boost our self-confidence with self-observation, do a self-analysis with a neutral perspective, keep an eye on the opportunities, get rid of the shortcomings, and attain a series of successes.

The secret of success: trust your intuition

In the third chapter, we have studied the five senses and the subconscious mind in great detail, known as the sixth sense in colloquial terms and as clairvoyance in spiritual terms. We have also studied that we can achieve the state of self-realization by enhancing the positive prowess of our subconscious mind through self-suggestion. We are also aware that this is the biggest asset, enabling us to witness all the opportunities and shortcomings from a neutral perspective. Why is it then that we cannot utilize our unlimited power source, the intuition, through which the knowledge always keeps flowing? Why can we not trust it? It is because we have not yet attained the stage of self-realization of our subconscious mind.

Yes! Read this segment repeatedly unless we acknowledge the importance of the subconscious mind, i.e., the capacity of our intuition; how can we awaken self-realization within ourselves. Unless this happens, how will we be able to trust our intuition? This is known as having faith in yourself, i.e., trusting your potential and opportunities. This trust should be unabated, have confidence in yourself (without ifs and buts). It is important to remind yourself what the success mantra Napoleon had discovered after researching successful people, as suggested by Andrew Carnegie. Belief is the key to success, the great secret to accomplishing the astonishing, a great formula, the tremendous divine weapon or the *Brahmastra* (the divine weapon of *Lord Brahma*).

This intuition is also known as the spiritual sense, which Kabir explained in his Doha:

कस्तूरी कुंडल बसे मृग ढूँढत बन माहि ।

ज्यों घट घट में राम हैं दुनिया देखत नाहि ।।

(Meaning: A deer has the fragrance in itself and runs throughout the forest to find it. Similarly, Ram is everywhere, but the world does not see him.)

So, how do we smell the divine fragrance which springs out continuously from our subconscious mind? What can we do to remove the lid from the source of fragrance so that the world also gets a chance to enjoy success in our lives?

Once we recognize our intuition, its scent will start flowing, and we will make decisions comfortably. The findings will be spontaneous, and the results will also be the same. Then we won't have to force our efforts to be successful, and everything will fall into place, and this will become our second nature. This is what we call self-devotion, praying to the lord with complete dedication. In *Geeta* Shri, Krishna teaches about performing our duty without any desire for the result; we can also call it natural artistry, our natural working capabilities.

Once we start using our common sense to make ourselves natural workers, we will realize the projects which can be materialized. Our subconscious mind starts making decisions, a clear indication of which reflects on our feelings. If the plan is correct, you will feel excited about it, and if it does not happen, it is better to shelve it and move forward. You should awaken and invest your energy in such projects that excite you and makes you believe in them.

Now is the time to rearrange and retrain your common sense, intelligence, intellect, and rationality and acknowledge that the knowledge stored in our subconscious is like an inexhaustible vessel. It is a store that is never empty. So, open the gates of your mind and acquire internal prosperity. This is the property that has been and will be with you forever and when you possess this, being wealthy is no big deal. You should train your intelligence/intellect/ senses to listen and respond to your intuitive voice.

The feeling that you get from your intuition is controlled by nature. When it rises with full impact, we develop self-discipline, and this self-discipline enables us to question our inner self, intuitive self, and authentic self.

So how do we decide the timing of decision-making? How will we know that we have done all the necessary preparations and research? The answer is straightforward, we need to trust our subconscious program, our inner self, and we should tell ourselves that the correct answer will come to us naturally. My inner guidance is taking me on the right path, or my internal forces enable me to make the right decisions. When we repeat these words repeatedly, we will be able to listen to the voice of our inner self. This should be listened to carefully. The words that seem natural are the answer; this is the authentic voice of our inner conscious. This is the correct direction. With this, we are calling for our intuitive mind or self-wisdom through information and confirmation. We need to decide, act and move forward with these words, directions, and commands. Our reflexive action is pre-defined, which means success is pre-decided.

When we start to live our lives on common sense, our brain synchronizes it with our soul, which means that our brain identifies our subconscious, and our decisions become natural. Our brain automatically starts editing the information that the five senses send to it in this condition. Then only the exact information reaches our subconscious; that is, only necessary information is stored on the hard disk of the brain's computer. Eventually, our software starts making the correct calculations.

If you feel difficulties making decisions using your common sense, you should give yourself a break. It can be momentary or for some hours or days, or even more than that. Give yourself time to review the facts, but it should not be more than necessary because it is essential to draw a timeline for fact review. This timeline will awaken your intuitive decision-making.

Of course, the ancient solution to this problem is 'a sleepover it'. There is an old saying sleep is the mother of all counseling. It is true that when we leave behind all our anxieties and go to sleep, our five senses are deactivated, the link of the outer world with our brain is disconnected, and then our subconscious mind starts working without any hindrance. Many problems, which seem unsolvable in the evening, disappear overnight. The morning light removes the darkness (troubles) of our brain. It looks as if there were no problems at all; only the unnecessary information had stopped their natural flow.

There is another foolproof technique. Whenever you are battling any problem, make a pros and cons list of all the possibilities and obstacles. It doesn't matter how simple this list might look; this writing process is very effective. It works as a balance, and you should decide to favor the heavier side. This list makes our decision-making very simple. If the balance is in equilibrium, leave the decision to your subconscious, and your intuition will find the right path. The equilibrium might also indicate that the possibilities can battle our obstacles. This means that our passion can overpower our fear, and we can achieve success. On the contrary, if your love is below average, the result will also be below average.

Now is the right time to decide

What is the gravest yet most common mistake in decision-making? We keep waiting for the right time and condition and miss the opportunity. This is an excuse. The right time starts right now. Every moment is precious because time is an asset that can't be reverted. Nature has our lifespan pre-determined, and it keeps on decreasing with every passing moment. This might sound pessimistic, but the unchallenged truth is that death is inevitable, and we move closer to our end every second. This is what Kabir said:

काल करे सो आज कर, आज करै सो अब ।

पल में परलय होयगी, बहुरी करेगा कब ।।

(Tomorrow's works, do today's work now; if the moment is lost, how will the work be done?)

So many successful people have walked this earth, and they might not have come across these lines from Kabir, yet this is the mantra they chant throughout their lives. They do not postpone today's work until tomorrow. The most crucial task for any person who wants to be successful is that he should understand the importance of time and assimilate it into his life and make it a part of his daily routine.

There is a story from Mahabharata about Karna in this context. Once Karna was sitting in his court, and a mendicant approached him. Karna was busy with his work at that time, so when he heard the mendicant's voice, he took out his pearl necklace from his neck by his left hand and gave it to him. One of his courtiers was watching this, and he objected to its saying that alms should not be provided by the left hand. Karna replied, 'when he asked for alms, I had nothing except my necklace around me, and my right hand was busy. It is possible that my mind would have changed if I had waited for my right hand to be free to give him something, and I would not have given him anything. Who knows what will happen in the next moment? That is why I gave him the necklace with my left hand.'

This is why Karna is known as the greatest benefactor of all time. You can realize now that a person who values every moment of his life will scale all heights of success. You can try it for yourself. All you have to do is that whatever you are doing should be completed now; do not procrastinate. Prepare a list of all the work you need to do in the day by their priority and start working on them. Try this for a few days, and you will realize how much precious time you had wasted waiting for the opportune moment. Also, as the cluster of pending works starts to clear off, your mental tension will begin to ease off. You will have more time for demanding jobs and require time. Once you can manage your time, you will start enjoying solving your problems. Work will become your worship, and you will become a devout worshipper of your heart and soul.

It would be best to remember that it is the opportune moment to work on whatever path-breaking thoughts you have cultivated in your dreams because you are not the only one who has developed those thoughts. Are you proud of your unique idea? Look at Google, and you will know. Many people have spent so much time working on it, and these results and searches have been stored while only a tiny fraction of information has been held there.

Your implementation might be different, but no particular performance mode can be successful forever. The reason is straightforward, and implementing an idea is done in various ways. It cannot be predicted when your vision will become someone else's idea in these conditions. Even if your concept and implementation are unique, you must act swiftly because the passion, which is very strong at this moment, might die down later, and that revolutionary project might stop.

This is why most successful people have developed the habit of making decisions and implementing them right now. They implement their ideas with passion and dedication. Even in today's digital world, when information is transferable in seconds, the doctrine of 'slow and steady wins the race' is applicable like a universal truth. The only condition is that this principle is a part of your strategy. And you are now applying it due to your weakness and laziness. Yes, this quote can also come true. Haste can hamper good advice, but when you make decisions through your common sense, it will not be a hasty decision, and when you implement it with all the energy and passion, its success will be predetermined.

Hence, 'Listen to all but do what you want.' Here also, caution is essential. It would help if you did not shut down your senses in the obsession with this statement. It would help if you accepted whatever comes naturally because whatever is the source of information, it becomes a part of our store once you receive it. Hence, one should dream with open eyes, but it is achievable. One should only see whatever your mind says. In other words, when you are calm, your eyes will see what your intuition can accept. This is what we call the unification of body and soul. And once you add your wealth – your energy, passion, and skills. When the idea is implemented with complete collaboration of body, soul, and assets, its success could be predefined.

It would be best if you also cared for many other things – stay firm on your decisions, do not give up easily, learn from past mistakes, etc. At this point, I would like to reiterate that once you make decisions by common sense and then implement it naturally, then mistakes won't happen, and even if they do occur, you can rectify them within time.

Summary

What do you want? Ask this straight to your subconscious. If the answer is more than one, then write them down. Allow your mind to calm. The best time to do this is when you go to bed. Very calmly repeat your questions and listen to your subconscious very carefully. You might not get the answer on the first attempt, but the second and third ones will give you your honest answers. However complicated the problem might seem, the capabilities of your subconscious are infinite, and every question put to it is very average.

Look for opportunities in your plans and ideas, even though the rest of the world might only see problems. Keep in mind that in every issue lays an option, and find them. If you feel that every time you start working on something new, a new problem crops up, just remember that you are learning something new, and you are moving ahead on the road to success.

Trust your instincts. This is the secret to success. The most straightforward trick to listening to your subconscious or availing its advice and instructions is to knock on its door twice every day. Pause, relax, synchronize your inner feelings and repeat your question. This is called knocking on the door of your subconscious. Listen carefully to those musical signals. You will get your honest answers, and then you should start working on them. Every step you take further will be a milestone on your journey to success.

❑

6

BEST WAY TO ACQUIRE WEALTH

"Take up one idea. Make that one idea your life-think of it, dream of it, live on that idea. Let the brain, muscles, nerves, every part of your body, be full of that idea, and just leave every other idea alone. This is the way to success"

—Swami Vivekananda

Great
Vedanta philosopher

"Don't aim for success if you want it; just do what you love and believe in, and it will come naturally."

—David Frost

English journalist, comedian, and writer

"Do what you love to do and give it your very best. Be it business or baseball, or the theatre, or any field. If you don't love what you're doing and you can't give it your best, get out of it. Life is too short. You'll be an old man before you know it"

—Al Lopez

Former major American league Baseball player and Manager

Do you also feel that you did not get the opportunity to become what you wanted? Most people say that. Some people say, 'I wanted to establish my own business, but I did not have the capital, skill, or talent.' Most people in the world are employed, and most are distressed by their jobs.

People often say, "I am fed up with my job. But since there is such a job crunch, I can't do the stupidity of quitting my job. What will I do if I can't find another job?" A vast majority of such people are also frustrated with their profession. You will find such people saying, 'I wanted to become a writer, but my father did not allow me, and I became a civil servant; I wanted to become a Doctor, but I would have to study too much. Therefore, I became a teacher, etc.'

Do what you love

More than half of the working population of this world is not satisfied with their present job. The multinational staffing company' 'Kelly services found out in a survey done across the globe with 1.20 lakh participants in 2103 that 47 percent of employees are not happy with their present job. This trend is more or less prevalent in every field: self-employment, business, or entrepreneurship. There is discontent in most people, which is why there are so many unsuccessful people worldwide. It is a hard truth that only a few can scale the heights of success.

What is more saddening is that unsuccessful people portray themselves as incapable, as if somebody had tied their limbs and shut their brains. They try to sympathize with different prologues as if they were injured and defeated by some compelling opponent. In the majority of cases, the reality is just the opposite. The words might seem harsh but such people are deserters, weaklings who fled the battlefield.

It is evident that we are distinguishing ourselves from such deserters, and we are trying to move forward on the path of success. So, have you ever asked yourself if you want to do what you are doing or going to do? What if some other work attracts you? Will you try it or continue doing what you are doing right now. It is essential to find answers to these questions; otherwise, the old saying 'grapes are sour' will be repeated to you.

There is still time; you should seriously ask yourself what you want to become? What is the most revered dream of your life? What do you love doing most? What is that thing for which you are ready to quit everything and still be happy? Not for some time, but forever. What is that job for which you are willing to risk everything? The desire to become successful is like having your passion for your lover, like Laila-Majnu, Heer-Ranjha, and Shirin-Farhad.

You can look at any successful person, and you will find that they are perseverant. His job is his life, his foremost priority for a successful person. They get irritated if they cannot complete their work for any reason. Nothing else interests them. They might appear restless at first glance, but this restlessness is due to their passion for their work. This restlessness is not like those of ordinary people. They are busy looking for new ways to finish their job. They are crazy about their work and do not like any interference in their job. They consider every obstacle a challenge and find immense pleasure in fighting and defeating their obstacles.

So what is the work that you enjoy doing most? How do we identify the work that we were born to do?

Look at the daily routine of any person who is discontent with their job or profession. You will be surprised to know the volume of such people. They work in different sections, and their lifestyle might differ, but their routine and ideology are identical. What is their lifestyle like? Since it is mandatory to work for at least eight hours, they enter the workplace, work half-heartedly to keep their job and flee the workplace after mandatory hours as if freed from jail. They reach home tired after roaming, chit-chatting, and bossing over their kids. They lecture their kids on work ethics, and if they indulge in any mischief, or if the wife reminds them of any domestic responsibility, they shout at them and sometimes even beat them and take out their frustration on them. They expect their kids to achieve and do everything that they failed at. They teach their kids to reach great heights in life.

These discontent people never compromise with their comfort or divertissement; they eat what they like, dress as they want, sleep for most of the time if not bound by their eighth hour duty time, and appear highly elated on Sundays and other holidays. With the passing day, they get gloomy about going to the office again in the morning. They drink to overcome their depression and are also involved in immoral activities. But these people have one virtue: they do not commit any crime because they cannot take risks. They also try to appear as gentlemen outside their home, but their pride is at unassailable heights. If you interrupt them, they reciprocate strongly, saying they are their masters.

Discontent people have some other qualities as well. They like and impart knowledge about everything apart from their job. They also have the hobby of reading, and they never restrict themselves from commenting on everything. They enjoy interrupting, making a fool out of others, and proving themselves wise. They also appear very logical. Whatever you ask them, they have the perfect logic (excuses). Of course, their reality came in front when the time to do something came. They are always attentive on every social-spiritual occasion but never take any responsibility. They consider avoiding work as an act of a wise and take immense pride in this skill. They think plagiarism to be artistry and are happy to do flattery in office politics. Finding faults in others is their specialty, while they don't have anything. If they don't get promoted, they don't make a scene and even appear satisfied on the outside, but jealous of those who do, and they won't let them go without a fight.

Our motto here is not to count the flaws in a discontent person but to make you aware of these passive and fortuitous ideologies if you want to succeed. Unfortunately, this ideology prevailing in a discontent person makes him even more discontent and entraps him in a mental trap. Therefore it is essential to get rid of these thoughts before they grow. Let us contemplate what may break loose if you quit your present job. You will be free of this trap and try to do what you want. Until we start the treatment, the disease will continue to rise. All you need to do is awaken your inner self and develop the passion for reshaping your life.

Take a step forward in the direction of your choice, and you will be so glad that the road ahead will become more accessible, and every moment you will feel victorious, which will multiply your passion manifold. Then you will not remain a burden anymore, and it will become the love of your life, and your life will become blissful. Wealth and success come to only those who can keep themselves happy. To please Goddess Lakshmi, you need to light the lamp of optimism in the temple of your mind, and once you do that, the darkness (pessimism) will be gone forever.

Life gives you what you believe

Do you know why most people cannot do what they regret all their lives? When you ask them, most of them will answer – that was only my dream, and I don't want it to materialize; I got what I deserved in reality. Not only this, but they won't even forgo a chance to advise you that you should keep your feet on the ground. In other words, do not dream. Of course, they got what they deserved-boredom, frustration, problems, and below-par income. If they had not dreamed of anything, how could they realize it?

The truth is that such people began killing their natural individual desires, inclinations, and ambitions right from the beginning because the statement that dreams never come true was fed into their minds by their parents, family, and society. This is why they never made any efforts to fulfill their desires, ambitions, and inclinations and are left with only memories. If they could not muster the courage at that time, then how could they do it now?

As we have studied earlier, one should be mentally prepared to fulfill his desires; he needs to challenge the circumstances and then materialize them with passion.

Is it now possible to awaken your dreams? Of course, yes! You must have come across the saying 'better late than never. Just accept that until now, you have awakened from a deep sleep just now. You must not sit back thinking it's too late and how will I climb this hill? Keep in mind that every step you take forward will bring you closer to your goal. Don't bother if you will be able to reach the top. Focus only on the fact that 'this is what I love to do. It gives me pleasure, and this is what I will do now and won't spend the rest of my life in frustration.' This only is the first step on the way to prosperity and wealth. Now you are doing what you wanted to do. The law of nature is that you can be successful only if you love what you do. Then why do something that makes you unhappy?

When you will do something happily, the results will be astonishing. You will be surprised at the volume of the work you can do. Not only is your energy saved but also your time. Now you will have ample time to learn new techniques, which will help fasten your pace of completing your job. When you work in a jolly mood, your efficiency will also increase. Your first goal will pave the way for the second one, and the second one will do so for the third one, and you will start expecting more from your life. Once you do that, life will give you what you desire, and this is the law of life.

Ignite your passion, and success will come looking for you

Until now, we have casually discussed the role of passion. Now let us dive deep into it and see its role in becoming successful. What is a passion, after all? It is the state of excitement of the deepest feelings of our mind. When does it arise? It ignites when we develop sincere feelings for any object, ideal (thought or work), or mindset (trust, faith, or belief). History is full of stories of passionate people. Be it a love story or any social, economic, spiritual, or cultural-historical incident, a hero is a passionate person in the center of all.

So do only a few particular individuals have passion? No, look closely inside yourself, and you will find passion. Have you ever tried to identify your passion? Unfortunately, most people do not know what their passion is, and if they do, they do not harness it. They do not do something that would ignite their passion, and are afraid of it and have kept suppressing it since childhood. It is something like when most people crush their dreams under the ideology of pessimism. When you chase your dreams, move forward toward your love, and fan your desires, your passion will ignite.

But, since childhood, we are fed the practical thought that desires do not let you remain a human; it makes you passionate to the extent that you will become crazy and selfish. This means that a passionate man becomes so crazy about his goal that he forgets his family and social responsibilities. He does not have time for anybody else, and he becomes selfish and thinks only of himself.

You will find such examples in most families. He who wasted his time in social bindings did not even realize when he fell behind in the race of life. Some children, out of many of the same parents, move far ahead while some lag behind; why? You will find that the successful one was perseverant from childhood and always indulged in his work; they did not have time for family or social activities. The exciting thing is that even the family members keep them away from such time-wasting activities. Since these passionate kids are bright students and become a hope for a better family's financial and social stature, the family also invests most of their resources and takes care of their every need.

But the actual problem arises when this kid grows to become successful and leaves behind his family members. The pursuit of success aspires to their passion of achieving more success, and they do not have time for their wife, children, and the relatives that were left behind to go even lower on their priority list, and as a result, they see him as selfish and crazy.

This is the rule of success. It does not come without cost. Unless the person desiring success goes mad, he cannot achieve it. To become successful, a man has to risk everything. When everything is left behind, then the natural desire emerges. Then he and his success become the same. That is why there is a saying A person is alone at the top. But the person on the top does not work only for himself. His efforts bring revolutionary results that better the lives of hundreds and thousands of people.

Why can't everybody ignite their passion? It is because they live for their parents and relatives instead of themselves. What is the result? They live neither for them nor for themselves. It is pretty clear that most people try to imitate the path of others and do not fan their passion. Every person has a different passion. You cannot master it unless you work on it. This is the true nature of passion. It brings out all the possibilities in a person, collectively known as a specialty. So, the true power of passion is directly proportional to your action. When there is no action, your passion goes to sleep. If you find that your passion is dormant, you will have to do what you love most to ignite it, and now that you have decided to become rich, you will have to do something which you can do with passion. This will become your specialty and distinguish you from the crowd on your way to success.

Radical thoughts and a bold personality is necessary

Formal education is not enough to become wealthy and successful; you need something else. Radical ideas and a bold personality are essential for this. The opportunities to achieve these in college and university are minimal; in fact, these are discouraged most of the time. The academic structure of most institutions is such that they tend to keep the students on one level instead of encouraging different thoughts in them. Due to this structural flaw, the course of study suppresses the creativity of students, which is the essential element in finding new possibilities and ideas to solve a problem.

The irony is that schools, parents, and society unknowingly also crush individual aspirations even before their budding. Since the process starts in childhood, we do not aspire to achieve anything significant in life even after growing up. Even if a thought crops up, we cannot muster enough courage.

These all result from faulty software programs installed in our subconscious in childhood. Instead of motivating us to chase new opportunities, they pull our legs, and it stops our aspirations, dreams, and ideas from expanding their wings.

The other problem is our surroundings, which are not encouraging, especially when young. As a significant section of our society suffers from a mediocre mindset, our friends are also the same; hence, we consider their practical ideology proper. Yes, most people acknowledge and teach reasonable beliefs. They accept what they can get quickly and easily get what is expected. We should work accordingly if we want to achieve something special. We must muster the courage to come out of our comfort zone and chase our dreams with all our energy.

Success is not served on a golden platter to anybody, and it is achieved by working hard and putting everything a stake. When you erase your past, you put everything on the stake, stand firm in the present, and move steadily towards the future. Creating the traditionalist and average mentality is what we can call reincarnation. That reincarnated man will be armed with rudimentary ideas and courage. He keeps moving forward on the path to richness and success (as per the directions of his intuition and discipline) with valor (which people often confuse with recklessness) along with his desires, inclinations, and aspirations and generates new rudimentary ideas.

So now repeat the mantra of success-whatever others might call me, crazy, selfish, or ambitious, now I don't care for anybody and will listen only to my soul and subconscious calls. This is what I was born to do. This will become the meaning of my life. Remember that our success is the success of self, it is the success of our soul, and the soul is omnipresent. It is present in every living being of this universe. Hence we are not selfish. We are self-devotees who listen to the call of our soul. We are working on the entire universe, and our acts are for the happiness and prosperity of all.

Once we start working with this attitude and move forward with our natural passion, we will run after success and wealth, but we won't stop for it and keep moving forward. Then our artistry, skills, and capabilities will become different from others and become rudimentary. This will change us into distinct personalities, and we will fulfill our duties towards society, country, and the universe. Our natural zeal will keep rising and intensifying our passion, and we will become passionate devotees. Work will become our worship. The goddess of wealth, Lakshmi, will enter the temple of our mind in her grand form. The entire abode will bathe in her radiance, and the great bells will ring in all directions.

Turn your desire into your resolution

As we have discussed earlier that only desire will not serve the purpose. Wishes are endless and infinite by nature. What is this desire? Our sense of yearning is born out of the aspirations of any person, commodity, or consequence. Such feelings are also an outcome of craving and desperation. When we yearn for any person or entity we desire, we are excited by its use and eager to attain our goal.

But due to a lack of willpower, our desires are not materialized in action. Former world champion car racer Mario Gabriele Andretti differentiates between desire and determination: "***Desire is the key to motivation, but most its determination and commitment to an unrelenting pursuit of your goal – a commitment to excellence – that will enable you to attain the success you seek.***"

You might have heard people saying that "I do not have any brilliant idea which I want to work on." This is a widespread complaint due to which most of them are confused. People trapped in confusion can never decide what they want and what kind of work is suitable for them, but the truth is that such people never ask their subconscious about their inner desires. This might clear off the confusion instantly. The subconscious will give directions and orders, which are naturally accepted.

What do we understand when people say they do not know what they want in life? They have only imitated others rather than listening to themselves, and they receive only failure and discontent. This is bound to happen if you cannot read your inner desires. But the real problem is, unless they ask their inner self, they will not know the answers to these questions. Unfortunately, these innocent people cannot awaken that feeling which would let them ask such questions. Why is it so? The answer is the same – the mind has the layers of the dust of presumptions that dreams do not come true, and all desires can never be fulfilled, which they unknowingly feed themselves growing in a pessimistic environment.

It is also evident now that one is unclear about what he wants to do in his life? What is his purpose in life? What can he do naturally or attain the necessary skills to do that? Then he cannot set clear-cut goals in his life? His chances of being successful are out of the question. In opposite to this, another universal truth is that even if we are transparent in our ambitions and can visualize our desires with absolute clarity, we will have to fulfill some conditions. What are these conditions which must be followed to achieve our goals?

If you closely examine the incidents of your life, you will be pleasantly surprised that those desires which were accurate and for which we had no hesitation, we achieved instantly. Can you remember the effort you had to put in for those desires? You won't remember much because the desires were natural, and so were the actions. This implies that we don't feel our efforts naturally to complete wild desires. Naturally, we do not know or feel any exhaustion from these tasks as our energy level does not decrease.

But there must be some weariness because both the mind and the body had put in efforts, but still, we feel nothing about it. Why is it so? It is because our subconscious is in synch with our brain and body. This is known as unrealized labor, meaning such work that did occur but did not feel like it. The point is that even if the struggle was spontaneous, it still was done by our brain and body. So there must have been some loss of energy. Absolutely yes! But our subconscious balanced this loss by generating a new form of energy-energy of joy. This is why natural charm compensated for the raw energy loss due to honest labor, and we received a gift of success and a bonus of genuine joy in achieving this success.

So now we can say that those ambitions, which are completely clear and devoid of any hesitation or complication, are easy to achieve. This is also a universal truth that such aspirations and desires generate in a limited volume. This does not mean that only a few people can develop such clear ambitions. Anyone can do it, but he will be put in a distinct category after this. But the number of people who can look into their subconscious and listen to it is pretty low. Most people are afraid to enter this deep into their subconscious because the roots of complexes like a failure and the impossible have become very strong. So they make unnatural efforts to fulfill deviant desires by imitating others. Due to this, they counter loss all the time, after which their complexes take the shape of mental cancer and become an incurable mental disorder.

But there is no reason to be sad. Since you have decided to become wealthy and successful, you are determined to determinate your negative complexes. Once again, go through the earlier chapters and do self-observation. It will let you know about your natural desire, making goal setting more accessible. Bear in mind that uprooting your complexes and clearing the dust of your subconscious is a very complex process. It will not happen instantly and will take some time. But you must carry on this process with patience, and you will start getting positive results. Gradually your confidence level will rise, and you will realize that you have come out of the mental crisis. You will be able to hear, understand and work on the voice and advice of your subconscious. You will begin to make decisions on that basis and move forward on the road to success. Then you will realize what you want in your life.

You can meet any successful person near you. You will find that they have absolutely no confusion about their aspiration and ambitions. They know what they are doing and why they are doing it. They know clearly, that whatever they are doing is natural because they have decided as commanded by their subconscious. When you look into their past, you will find that whatever they are doing today has profound roots. They work stubbornly on any project, but every new assignment connects to the earlier assignments. This means that their present success is a chain of small successes they have attained in the past. They were very clear about their ambition from a very early age and had worked nonstop. When you look deep into their lives, you will know that they had taken the help of their intuition to attain this magical success.

So when you do something under the command of intuition, your desire and intention are clear, transforming into determination. Then you can work with a passion, which results in success and forms a series of it.

Summary

- **Imagine your life as you want it to be. However, it might be today:** if you cannot do so, make a list of what you love with as many inputs as possible. Now analyze every point in detail and examine if the obstacle is valid. Remember the statement of Henry Ford:"if you think you can do a thing or think you can't do a thing, you're right."

- **What would you like to do if you had enough money:** if you would like to continue what you are doing today, you are on the right track because you are emotional and passionate about your job. If you would not do what you are doing right now, you should immediately look for other options. It would be best to ask your subconscious; you will get the honest answer and realize that it is the most loved job for you, and you can do anything for it.

- **Are your ideas rudimentary, and do you have the courage to do anything for them:** once again, take your subconscious's help? Specialty can only be achieved in something you love, which will become rudimentary. You will not feel tired but joyful in doing that. Continue with that job, and success is guaranteed.

- **Can you transform desire into grit:** when you work on the command of your intuition, then whatever you are doing will be your natural desire. You will be very clear about what you want and why you want it. So, when intentions are clear alongside desire, it will take the form of determination or grit and gradually strengthen.

Repeat the golden words of the inner self

- I am unique. I am me, and I am born to do what I do.
- I must remain myself. It is my birthright as well as duty.
- I am successful, and I will institute the goddess of prosperity and wealth in the temple of my mind.

❑

7

MAGIC OF GOAL AND WORK PLAN

"Arise, awake and stop not till the goal is achieved. Don't worry if you do not succeed, do not give up, keep trying. Take lessons from past mistakes and continue your struggle. Fortune favours the brave and diligent. Do not look back. Infinite courage, passion, power and patience is required then only the work will be completed."

—Swami Vivekananda

Great Vedanta philosopher

"Obstacles are those frightful things you see when you take your eyes off your goal."

—Henry Ford

Founder, Ford Motor Company

"To succeed in your mission, you must have single-minded devotion to your goal."

—A.P.J. Abdul Kalam

Space Scientist and former Indian President

Once we find our natural desire, passion, and the field we want to succeed in, we can only concentrate on our action plan. Interestingly, only a few plans are easy to act upon out of many. Thomas Peters and Robert Waterman have made excellent comments on the paradox of simplicity in their international bestseller on business management– 'In Search of Excellence.

Peters and Waterman have had the opportunity to closely study many managers' working styles while working for a multinational management-consulting firm–'McKenzie & Company.' These thinker consulting managers have found that most managers, especially those with a master's degree in business management or equivalent, could be vigilant towards their excellent work. These alert persons continuously change their course based on their expected value equation trends. They are the same people who can juggle through hundred variable models at their convenience; they make the roadmap of a complex incentive system; they are those who put in the pieces of the matrix structure. They carry the 200 pages strategic plan and 500 pages market requirement document, which is nothing more than the primary step in a series of product development exercises.

Peters and Waterman have made sarcastic comments about the competent MBA-trained managers and put them in the dumb category. They mention that our friends from this category are different. It is just that they cannot understand why every customer cannot be given personalized service, not even in the business of potato chips. They feel humiliated personally when the beer served to them turns sour. They cannot understand that the regular outflow of a new product is not possible, and that is why an executive cannot make suggestive inputs every few weeks. But the fact is that people with common sense can also solve these problems. Peters and Waterman conclude that although simplicity seems a negative term, those who run some of the best companies are simple to some extent.

It means that common sense can solve even the most complex problems. The reality is that issues are not as complicated as they seem. It is good to attain a specialty in something but make the right decisions. Common sense plays a role more critical than specialty, which is a common trait of successful people, whatever field they might belong to. They solve even the biggest problems in simple ways while the specialists remain trapped in its complexities. Therefore apart from the clarity in goals, a simple plan of action is essential to becoming wealthy and successful.

We need a good dose of innocence and simplicity if we want to believe that we can acquire this sum of money, if we're going to trust our dreams and if we're going to discard the negative people. People who are too much logical and intelligent can be successful, but their intelligence can limit their success if it limits the boundaries of their dreams.

Clear goals are significant

We began the previous chapter with the quote of Swami Vivekananda: "*Take up one idea. Make that one idea your life – think of it, the dream of it, live on that idea. Let the brain, muscles, nerves, and every part of your body be full of that idea and leave every other idea alone. This is the way to success.*" We need to repeat these words and examine ourselves if we implement them. Have we selected that one idea from our subconscious, which would be our ultimate goal? If yes, then have we tried to implement it in our life? If we have attempted to, then is this idea synchronized with our breaths? Do we only think about that idea while we are awake? Do we dream about this idea while we are asleep? Is its fragrance oozing out of every pore of our body and making us crazier and crazier to reach the topmost point of its success?

If yes, we can assume that we have selected the right goal, which is the path to our success. Walking on this road will take us to prosperity. The only condition is moving forward with patience : without tiring, without stopping, and without caring about winning or losing. This is our path to inexhaustible prosperity, supreme goal, and bliss. On this path, work transforms into worship. Like Kabir found his god in his weaving works, Raidas found his lord in his job at the tannery, and like a partridge, he is not afraid to risk his life to touch the moon. Once we find our goal, our lives become a journey, and we become travellers, success and prosperity become milestones, and we keep moving towards our supreme goal. Gradually even the memories of dreams fade away, and life and purpose become the same. Swami Vivekananda is trying to tell us : "*Arise, awake and stop not till the goal is achieved.*"

Look closely and find what is common in people around you? Only one thing is lacking in all of the them – Clear goals. Therefore, most people are unable to achieve anything significant in their lives. They are unaware of their purpose in life. They start doing whatever they can find. They do not have any ambitions. Many people did identify their goals but got scared of entering the deep and halted their journey midway. Such people who attain mediocre success create the biggest hurdle in the path of those who dream big. They are happy to be the one-eyed king in the land of blinds and give negative lectures based on their practical experience. They are hypocrites and jealous and try to stop everybody who tries to surpass them. They are aware of the path to success but lack the courage to walk on it because of their cowardice. This is why so many people become highly pessimistic in old age and start behaving like lunatics.

You will find only a few people who appear content with their life; because they are clear about their goals. Some might be rich while others are average, but they are all equally positive. They become standards in their respective fields. They are elated by the success of others as much as they are with their own. Their care for everyone and do not think ill of anyone. When you go close to them, you will find that whatever they have done is part of a plan. They do not copy others but do what they want to do. They will tell you that they had identified their goal in life and continued moving forward with available resources. They will say, 'we got what we had planned, nothing more, nothing less.'

The story of a salesperson is repeated in many business literatures who could not sell more than a particular amount. When his sales manager sent him to sell in an area where the possibility was very low, he made the sales of almost the exact amount as he did in the area with very high sales possibility. His confusion was his self-observation and goal. He never had faith that he could sell more, and this thought was embedded in his subconscious. He achieved more than expected sales in the area with low possibility, while he achieved less than expected in an area with high possibility. Neither more nor less.

This confusion is not confined only to the salesperson but happens to us. Just do a sincere analysis of your past experiences; you will realize that whatever you have achieved was directly proportional to the goals that you had set, neither more nor less. You got only as much as you desired, planned for, and made efforts for it. Whoever he might be, if the goals are unclear or undecided, or if he does not have any goals, the results will be the same, ambiguous, doubtful, or none. On the contrary, if someone establishes a clear purpose and implements it distinctly, he achieves it.

Why is it so? The answer lies with you, in your subconscious. You will get the results based on the realistic goals you set up according to your intuition and the type of software program you feed into your brain. It is not a surety that you will have to work hard to achieve your goals. You might achieve it quickly. Success was measured regarding hours put in labor in the past, but it was a mental game even back then and today. Hard work is the key to achieving any goal, but when you align yourself with your goal, abandon all the negativity, and install the program of achieving your goal in your subconscious, you get the desired result very quickly. Yes, better results can achieve with fewer efforts. Those who scale the heights of success are aware of this simple but universal truth. Even if this is secret, you can experience it by setting clear goals. You can see the secret door opening as soon as you place your goals naturally, and you will reach your destination moving on this path.

It would be best to be careful as the number of people with unclear goals is relatively high even in the community of hard-working and goal-oriented persons. Most people get content with a minor betterment of their life without considering that they can achieve it if they set solid goals for an ideal life. This means that if your goals are not clear, you will not be able to reach the point where you could have with a little more effort.

So what is your goal for the next year? How much do you want to earn–5 lakhs, 50 lakhs, one crore, or even more? If you're going to bring a considerable change in your life : a completely genuine desire, then ask yourself what should be your aim? If you want a bright future, then set your goals and decide the energy and time you are willing to and capable of devoting to achieving it. If you dream only about a promotion or a better job prospect and have not set any distinct goal, the miracle you desire won't happen. Bear in mind that your self-worth can only be as much as you consider it.

Every successful person acknowledges this fact. If you set clear goals and keep riding every visible step of the ladder (it should be those which can convince your subconscious about your sincerity), you will realize that you have reached your destination.

Do not underestimate yourself

Most people's biggest mental block on themselves is in their minds. It is an interesting psychological fact that we cannot estimate our worth correctly. One should always keep in mind that a person's net worth is exactly what he assumes, neither more nor less. Even though he may appear self-confident but most people underestimate themselves. The number of those people who know their inner self and consider themselves valuable is significantly less. There is a hint of inferiority complex in every person, which is why he does not consider himself worthy to reach those heights of success he is capable of. As a result, most people limit their success and prosperity due to an inferiority complex.

Now the question arises how do we get rid of this inferiority complex and do a correct valuation of ourselves? The best way is to develop our self-esteem. We have already discussed transforming the thought of an individual in earlier chapters. Hence the best way to strengthen and build your self-esteem is to work with a specific monetary objective. Unless we equate our work with money, we will not know our true worth. Whatever field we might be working in, measuring self-esteem regarding money is very important.

The magical effect of annotated objective

We are confused while setting our distinct monetary objectives or goal. However confident we might try to appear, there is a hint of doubt in our subconscious, limiting our desires' clarity. Hence, our first objective should be to "be realistic'; after we achieve this first objective, setting the next more significant goal becomes easier for us. Of course, it is essential to draw the boundary of the second objective. Those who put their dreams clearly for the first time realize that not only they were able to achieve them, but they had moved ahead of them.

It also shows that you had set your goal way lower than your capabilities, and when you achieve it, you realize that you could have achieved more. Therefore, the second objective should be more significant enough to seem unrealistic initially, but it is essential to challenge yourself. Otherwise, you won't be able to realize your true capabilities. Now you must start working on your second objective with absolute passion. It is an exciting game that brings very profitable results. You should not be surprised if you achieve your target in six months instead of one year that you had assumed. Such are the miraculous results of clear objectives.

Once again, this proves how low you had estimated your capabilities, but this is how self-estimation works. Now that you have achieved desired results for the second time, your next objective becomes clearer. Ultimately you can do a precise valuation of yourself, and your purpose brings you desired results, neither more nor less.

Your possibilities are infinite

It is not an exaggeration but a universal truth that your value is immeasurable, way higher than your calculation; the only problem is that no one might have told you this. The irony is that many close people you might have repeatedly told you the opposite, that your value is much lower than you think.

Be careful! It would be best if you remembered that intelligence, work, motivation, imagination, discipline, and experience are significant success factors. But you might have also seen that despite having all these, many people do not become successful; even if they do, it is only a mediocre one, or they do not live up to their capabilities. It might be happening to you as well. You may have many skills, and you might be putting in all the efforts, but still, success slips out of your hands. You might know many people from your workplace who are not as talented as you, but still, they manage to move ahead, be promoted, and achieve envious success.

Why? Take a close look at their activities and lifestyle. You will realize that their self-image has decided their goals, and their plans have decided their lifestyle. Now look at yourself; what is the difference between you and those moving ahead, being promoted, and achieving extraordinary success. It is essential to understand this difference. Feel your shortcomings with a very calm mind; you will realize that you had committed a grave mistake, and that mistake was that you had underestimated yourself. Yes! You had not measured your capabilities accurately, i.e., you did not do your correct self-imagination. Your objective was affected, and this wrong objective restricted the result or your success. Now its impact is projected on your lifestyle.

You had everything apart from the essential quality: accurate self-estimation. What are you thinking now? Unless you remove this mental block and increase your self-estimation is having faith in your capabilities, your objective will not grow, and hence the results will not be significant. Be calm and look in your subconscious. You will get an accurate answer, and you will be able to expand your objective. Once the bells of self-confidence start tolling in the temple of your mind, you will be able to see success in all directions. This only is the power of the subconscious, your capabilities, and the power of your soul.

So wake up and hold the arms of your trust and joyfully start walking on the path towards success and prosperity. You won't feel any fatigue, and you will cross your goals one after another. Every plan will raise your self-confidence, and you will be able to increase your self-estimation. The goal will keep getting bigger. Your passion will become grander, and your lifestyle will start competing with itself. All the powers within your subconscious will awaken, and you will feel the limitless, endless, and infinite power inside yourself. This is also known as self-awareness in the spiritual world, and a self-aware person is capable of making accurate decisions, setting precise goals, and ensuring desired outcomes.

Make your objectives your only definite idea

Objectives work like magnifying glasses. It converges all the powers of one idea to bring desired results, just like a magnifying glass converges the sunrays into one point to create fire. Therefore we have to make our premier goal our only common definite idea. It has many positives. A concrete idea enables us to raise the bar of our capabilities and success and checks our energy from scattering in case of a mistake. When your definite objective transforms into the actual idea, success becomes inevitable.

Concentrating on a definite idea enables us to manage our personal and professional life to attain outstanding results even with less effort. We need to surround ourselves with those who complement our energy, stay away from those who detract us from our goals under such circumstances, and concentrate on our goals; how do we identify the things that help us and those that interfere with our efforts?

Our subconscious is the only administrator who tells us everything through common sense, and it will help us in this part as well. Whether we are selecting any partner, analyzing a friend's comments, reading any quote from a motivational book, or hearing the echoes of the truth of our records. You only have to ask your subconscious, and it will advise you, command you, and all you have to do is listen to it and implement it.

Things that you should bear in mind

- ❖ Write down your earnings goals for the next year on paper. You will realize that it was achieved in a much less expected time, i.e., you had underestimated yourself.
- ❖ Make the second objective larger than the previous. You will find that even this was very low concerning your capabilities. You must bear in mind that your goal should be realistic enough for your intuition to accept it.
- ❖ Finally, you will realize that your possibilities are limitless, and you will achieve any goal you set up through your common sense.

Chart a firm plan of action

The co-founder of Hewlett-Packard says, 'The decision of focussing on our efforts plays a vital role not only when a company is founded but also in later days.' The most crucial point in our journey is strategizing every step of our plan of action so that our objective takes a firm shape. There are possibilities that the result of being different or completely different from the expected outcome. But if we make our purpose unabashed and robust, we will achieve the desired results.

Unfortunately, many works do not pay substantial monetary dividends; therefore, it is better not to expect great economic results from such tasks. Still, if you want financial security and accumulate resources to chase your dreams, you must change your work. But you must cautiously examine your possibilities in depth before selecting such tasks. If it comes naturally to you and is by the command of your intuition and brings you joy, then there is no need to change it. But if you can squeeze your task a bit more, you can earn more money from it. Although the financial rewards in that job will be less than in other work, you will still get self-satisfaction. If it is not so, then look for such work and indulge in it with full passion and dedication only after approval from your intuition. This new job will bring you self-satisfaction as well as financial security.

Remember that no human being is infallible, not even the most experienced in business or any field, nor are those who have scaled the highest point of success. Everybody makes mistakes, and only those people who do not do anything at all never make mistakes, those who are inert, sluggish, and lazy. You will reach your goal despite temporary hiccups if you have installed the correct software program in the computer system of your subconscious. This is the true power of a work plan, harnessed through the right monetary goals and time-frame.

Stepwise plan of action and firm objective

What is the stepwise plan of action after all? It convinces your subconscious that your desire, dreams, aspirations, and ambition have become your objective. Stepwise, a plan of action is evidence that you have made a firm decision and are determined to achieve your definite goal, and you are preparing to counter every obstacle with a passion that comes your way in this journey. When your decision convinces your subconscious, it gets on this job with its limitless capabilities, and you can do what you are determined to do, neither more nor less. Implementing your plan of action could also mean taking the risk that arises due to our insecurities, especially when implementing our work plan with an obvious goal. In these conditions, every change, even for our betterment, creates a sense of insecurity. Personal security is so essential for most people that they are ready to sacrifice their dreams. You must remember that victory lies beyond fear. Never let your insecurities influence your dreams, and move forward with courage. Your real goal is only a few steps away. You will never have to repent this decision. We do not remember those who were afraid of the problems and turned back instead of crossing the bridge, but the world remembers those who moved forward with courage and achieved their goal. If there is any gap between victory and failure, then it is this bridge of personal risk. That is why this saying– *'Those who seek will find, but one needs to dive deep. I was scared of drowning, so I stayed sitting on the shore'.*

In our opinion, any individual should not set more than two goals in one field throughout their life at the same time. We could lose focus if we chase multiple goals at one time, affecting our work. But we can focus on various goals simultaneously if they belong to different fields, like professional qualifications, domestic work, physical qualifications, reforms in personal relations or research-related work, or completing a book can be done simultaneously, which develops our personality ultimately.

Another very fruitful action is an assignment of our future goals. We can set our goals for one year, five years, ten years, 20 years, or 50 years. Where do we want to reach when we are 60 years of age? What kind of person will we be when we are 80? What kind of life do we dream of? What will be our physical and mental condition? Do we want kids? If yes, then how many and how will they be brought up? Finally, what do we want to accomplish in our life? Be alarmed that you should not underestimate yourself. Keep in mind that your possibilities are limitless, and you will get as much as you sincerely desire, neither more nor less. Therefore sit down with a calm mind and prepare your plan of action as per the order of your intuition. Usually, people make plans and forget their goals. Our advice will be to live your goals every moment of your life and never let them out of your sight.

We are the architect of our life castle. We can change our future, even though we may have spent most of our lives earlier in failure, whatever our age because we are the architect of our life castle. Yes! We can take lessons from past mistakes and invest every moment of our present in building our future. It is still with us; what is gone is gone. Repenting it is nothing but losing precious moments of our life. Let us forget our past and start realizing our present to achieve the goal in the future. Most people realize their real purpose in life in the 60th or 70th decade and still accomplish it. Hence there is no age to realize your dream. Start chasing it whenever you recognize it, and remember that no ambition is more prominent than man.

When we draw a road map of our ideal future, when we know what we want to do in our lives, our short-term goals become clear and meaningful. Then we gain a reason to wake up every morning, and every step we take towards our goal reduces the distance between us and our purpose. Then every action becomes meaningful, the pace keeps increasing, and we can see our goal clearer than before. Yes! Then we can see how our future will take shape, and our every action starts to identify itself with it. This is the process known as writing one's future; to be one's fortune maker.

When you learn the art of portraiture of your life, make an accurate image of an ideal situation to shape your future as you desire. This also happens because we can install the correct software program through creative witnessing and positive dreams in our subconscious. It is an exciting situation. A natural alignment occurs between our conscious and subconscious minds. Then we start to portray our life naturally, and the control of our future comes into our hands. This is when we become the architect of our life, the creator of our destiny, and the blueprint of the entire life plan becomes an image of our future goal.

Our long-term goals not only define the ideals of our life but also help in shaping them. They make choosing one correct option much easier for us. Otherwise, they look very complex and confusing. Choosing the right path becomes very difficult in a lack of long-term goals, and this is why many people wander off in the wrong direction after walking on the correct way for some time and deviate from their dreams. Not only this, but they also make bad decisions in everyday life because of this deviation. They are unable to differentiate the wrong from the right. Whatever seems right at the moment, they do it, and the outcomes could be dangerous. Therefore every step we take should be in the direction of our fundamental goal, and this is possible only when we can set it correctly.

It is interesting that the process of goal setting, which looks very complex in a cursory look, is thrilling and motivating and contributes to every aspect of our lives. We must stay cautious that setting long-term goals does not mean that it won't require any modifications from time to time. Yes! We should keep our goals flexible because constant adaptation is essential to maintain the flow of life and keep moving forward. It is not sure that the conditions will be as expected today when we reach the fifth or tenth year of our goal; if we are chasing our dreams naturally and developing our capabilities following new requirements, then we might get our goals much earlier and much easier than we had expected

There is a solid reason for this as well. When our subconscious is armed with accurate programs, the new conditions are far better than our expectations or past experiences. Every day we come across new and better states. As we keep developing, our absolute possibilities are realized more and more, and the dreams get bolder, more ambitious, and most costly. We often discard some of our fundamental dreams mid-way because when we had set them, our mindset was not big enough, and in the present, they become irrelevant. Therefore, as our thinking grows, the result gets grander, success gets grander, and we continue moving towards the attainment of more and more self-fulfillment and personal enrichment if they are a part of our goals.

Now is the time to carefully design a primary goal for next year. It is also essential that we keep ourselves flexible to be aware of excellent opportunities in the future that we cannot see today. We should have a clear work plan to achieve our target, and annual goals should be turned into monthly goals and monthly and weekly goals. A firm plan of action saves us from delays and anxiety and keeps us moving towards our goal.

Your character is your destiny

A famous quote from a pre-Socratic Greek philosopher, Heraclitus, is, 'A man's character is his fate. An individual's character combines his psychological specialties and behavior, which distinguishes him from others. An individual's destiny or future or fate is a combination of predestined events of his life, which is beyond his control or power. Then how does our character become our fate?

Determining life goals is very good and appropriate. It is essential for every person who aspires to be successful but to continue working on this every day, we need discipline, and the best discipline is the one that we impose on ourselves. It validates Heraclitus's statement that a man's character is his fate. If we look at people around us closely, we will find that this rule applies to every human being inequality without any exception. You will find that every successful man or woman possesses strong character and is highly disciplined. Nobody has become successful with the strength of character. Hence, becoming your own master and taking your fate into your hand is extremely important.

We do not mean the rigorous work schedule that throws out rest and imagination from our lives when we refer to discipline, nor are we encouraging the act of keeping yourself immersed in work all the time. The literal definition of discipline is training that can create a unique character or pattern of behavior, especially moral and psychological reforms. Individual discipline means that an individual should also take some time to rest out of his daily routine. He should exercise, tend his body, complete his family commitments, have time for enjoyment, and in the end, also stay alone at times.

Excess work, working more than your capacity, can never be productive. But one should remember that everybody has different capabilities; it is very likely that the volume of work, which is too much, could be expected of somebody else. Therefore, despite comparing your working capacity with others, it is better to work at your natural power. Your natural ability is one, which allows you to work until you are not tired, and does not bore you. It does not mean that you underestimate yourself; act in a balanced way; neither way nor less.

By the way, working too much is in fashion these days. To climb the ladder of success, people work day and night, but when you analyze their root feelings, you will find they treat it as their compulsion, and this compulsive attitude is the factor that prevents them from achieving success. Such people do not achieve anything but desperation because they don't do their work naturally. They are fakes who act as if they are working in the greed of promotion or salary hike and keep themselves in the good books of senior officials. They often fail in their actions because fake works do not bring accurate results. The truth is that successful people do not work to please others; they work because they like working, and it is their natural work, which is evident to others.

Success is a habit

When we discipline ourselves in coordination with our natural capabilities and install positive programs in our subconscious, it also helps develop our self-rule and style of working; it searches for the working ground and structure and creates a habit of success inside us. This habit of success starts to uproot the patterns of failure, and mediocre result-oriented practices and success become a forced or second habit for us. This means that when we work on the command of our intuition and achieve self-discipline, then success becomes unstoppable and is attracted to us from all directions. It is a condition when our subconscious creates a magnetic force in our personality, known as the waking of inner power.

That is why an old saying is still valid, 'when you sow an idea, you will reap an action; When you sow an action, you will reap a habit; when you sow a habit, you will reap a character when you sow character you will reap a destiny.'

These words contain the power to change the flow of our lives and enable us to think like prosperous billionaires. We are armed with all the necessary information to walk the road to success. Our destiny is in our control, so pick up a pen, write down your goal and objective, chalk your stepwise plan of action, and indulge in implementing it. Whenever you are confused or troubled, then repeat the following mantra from Vrihadarnyaka Upanishad

अहं ब्रह्मास्मि (I AM BRAHMA)

Meaning– I am Brahma, or I am an infinite reality.

(अहं = I, Self-Pride, nobody can think that he does not exist.

ब्रह्म = Almighty, Omniscient, Omnipresent; that force out of which everything, even the Gods, is created.

अस्मि = am, the feeling and determination to exist)

What is the real meaning of I AM BRAHMA, and why are we stressing about pronouncing it repeatedly to become successful and think like a billionaire? In every chapter of this book, you have read many comprehensive statements, but in the end, it is essential to understand that we are Brahma. No other mantra teaches about our infinite capabilities. First of all, we must acknowledge that we exist. We should not consider ourselves inferior, incapable, and trim for any reason, perception, or anybody's views. This also is like denying our existence and a kind of suicide; if someone tries to convince you that you are not capable, then think of them as insane and ignore their words. The other point is that everybody is capable of doing anything, everything.

Addressing someone as Brahma means that a person has infinite capabilities, and it is equally present inside everybody. You are almighty. It is essential to self-experience Brahma, i.e., eternal reality. Guru Shukracharya, the commentator of Upanishads, also known as the conclusion of Vedas, tells us that a human being is almighty, and his personality is grand. Therefore, O Humans, give importance to your personality and trust your self-confidence; you are powerful– arise, awake, and ready to achieve what looks great. He who does not trust himself is poor and penurious, unsuccessful and his birth has no purpose on earth. Therefore the meaning of I am Brahma is that all of us have all the qualities to become successful and wealthy. When we work on anything acknowledging this, our success is predestined.

In the end, the sermon of Shri Krishna in Geeta given on working without expectation, human birth, and attainment of the absolute is also significant:

कर्मण्येवाधिकारस्ते मा फलेषु कदाचन।

मा कर्मफलहेतुर्भूर्मा ते सङ्गोऽस्त्वकर्मणि॥

You have the right to work only but never to its fruits. Let not the fruits of action be your motive, nor let your attachment be to inaction.

❑